THE NATURALIST'S
BEDSIDE BOOK

The Naturalist's Bedside Book

'BB'

Illustrated by
D. J. Watkins–Pitchford A.R.C.A., F.R.S.A.

Merlin Unwin Books

This edition published by Merlin Unwin Books Ltd (2008)
First published in Great Britain by Michael Joseph Ltd (1980)

Published by: Merlin Unwin Books Ltd
               Palmers House
               7 Corve Street
               Ludlow
               Shropshire SY8 1DB UK

               www.merlinunwin.co.uk

ISBN 978 1 906122 04 1

Typeset in Bembo by Anderson Technology.
Printed by Biddles Ltd, King's Lynn, Norfolk.

To

DES, MIONE and DI

For the Golden Years

CONTENTS

The wonder of the world,
The beauty and the power,
The shapes of things,
Their colours, lights, and shades,
These I saw.
Look ye also while life lasts.

The above inscription was copied from a north-country tombstone
by BB's father and reproduced in all the writer's books.

AUTHOR'S NOTE

I would like to thank the Editor of the *Shooting Times* for allowing me to include these extracts from my regular contributions to that paper. It is really in response to the numerous readers who have written to ask if these might be published in book form, and I have also added some extra pieces hitherto unpublished.

It is a book designed for casual reading and deals with many aspects of natural history and the countryside. I only hope it will bring a breath of the open air to those who have to live in our cities and towns. Each year the English countryside is shrinking at an alarming rate with the spread of new towns and fast highways, and the time may come when those who know and love nature as I do will be driven to the Highlands and border lands of England and Wales to find the wild life, the flowers, birds, and woodlands which some of us can still enjoy.

'BB'

The publishers would also like to thank James Fraser for kindly allowing us to add for the first time the 'BB' illustration of the Bowcase Stone (see page 101) to this edition of *The Naturalist's Bedside Book*.

WINTER

Winds of Winter

I like to hear the pipe of the wind in my bedroom window these winter nights. Perhaps rabbits in their holes, and hedgehogs and badgers in their nests share my view in these matters. There is something satisfying in being warm, tucked up, and wide awake, when outside the wind raves across the miles of countryside. I can imagine it sending the grey ripples chasing into the dead reeds on the lake, the great oaks flailing their arms in the lonely forest rides, the dead leaves whirling upwards into the darkness.

The sound of the wind brings back to me mental pictures of wild days and nights on the coast, the Solway whins at Carlaverock and Kingston tossing their cordlike branches, and the roar of the tide continuous and menacing, and, faintly on the wind, the yapping of the barnacle packs. In time long ago I used to crawl after them in the moonlight, hearing their low buzzing sound like a swarm of bees as they guzzled on the fine grass of the merse. In the high wind the clouds sped over the moon, flying shadows which, from time to time, broke suddenly to reveal the greenish ghostly landscape and the chasing icy ripples on the merse flood flashes, where the bright wigeon loved to come under the moon.

And again, the play of light and wind on the great reed beds on another estuary, that strange rushing and hissing and swaying of the plumed heads which bowed before each sudden onslaught. What difficult shooting it was, too, when the geese and duck came in with the gale behind them! On one such morning I saw my old fowling pal, Major Oakey, bring down seven geese one after the other, and Arthur Cadman, lying on his back among sugar-beet (or was it turnips?) knocking down a grey out of a party which came over at x miles an hour, right over his head.

One morning last November, during my goose hunt, we had such a wind which sent the leaves flying past me horizontally

3

and tossed the geese all ways. I do not like shooting in these conditions.

Enough of these rather pointless musings (I am typing, you see, to the sound of the wind outside the window, where the solemn Irish yews are bowing and bending). I have been mystified lately by a hen house sparrow which comes each day and taps urgently on my dining-room window. There is a creeper growing outside, a clematis (*Jackmanii*) and it sits on this, close to the window, and hammers on the glass. I think it must have a message for me, and I am a little uneasy about it. Long ago in my childhood when an elder brother was dying at school (the fact was concealed from me at the time) a pied wagtail came each day and fluttered at the schoolroom window. It was winter time, there were no flies about, and these wagtails were a rarity in our part of the midlands. This little sparrow, which seems fat and well fed, shows no fear of me, even when I go close to the window. I shall be glad when she has gone.

Last night a farmer friend rang me up to tell me that there has been a green 'macaw' flying loose in the woods by his farm. It has been about 'since harvest' so he said and chatters and scolds whenever it sees him walking with a gun. It is larger than a pigeon. This bird must be an escapee or wanderer from Lilford some six miles distant, for there the parrots fly about quite freely and nest in barrels in the trees. They have some good things at Lilford and it is well worth a visit, if only to see the magnificent snowy owls which are surely the most attractive of all the owl family. Their eyes are not huge like those of the tawny and long-eared, and they regard one with contemptuous stares out of their catlike barley-sugar optics with the fierce black iris. All the birds of prey have these merciless eyes, quite unlike those, say, of the duck tribe.

With daughter Angela, I went the other week to Peakirk near Peterborough. It was a dour autumn day. Men were burning leaves in the grounds and a dense choking pall of sweet-smelling smoke was blowing over the ponds, though the wildfowl did not seem to mind. I missed seeing greylags and could not spot a pink, but no doubt they were somewhere about. There was a very high wind blowing that day, too, and the pinioned duck were very excited and kept trying to take off against it and taking some tumbles in the process, very frustrating. The fantastic beauty and design of the duck family is delightful; it is difficult to say which is the most artistic in shape and plumage.

Some of the Cape geese were very tame, coming to feed out of our hands. It was so amusing to feel their warm bills shovelling up the grain in the palm of our hands. Each feather, too, exactly in place, all looking so sleek, happy, and well. We have much to thank Sir Peter Scott for; he must have given pleasure to thousands by his fine collection of the wildfowl of the world. The very small pygmy duck are almost unbelievable for they are so tastefully plumaged, and tame as well, toddling after one as one walks along the winding paths. The whole set-up is exceedingly well done and so well looked after. I was last there in the summer on a day of hot sun and watched a very ponderous carp swimming gravely round the pond just by the warden's cottage. But it was not visible the other day, for the water was clouded and rippled by the wind.

What a dreary time is this for the keen gardener. The late John Moore, the nature writer, whom I knew well, as I often broadcast with him, told me that the only time his garden looked really neat and pleasing was in the spring when all the seeds were in, the earth raked to a nice tilth, and all the rubbish of autumn out of the way and no plants showing. I have more or less given up any hope of tidying up my garden until all the leaves are down. They blanket the pond and the moorhens swim about, pushing them aside as they go. The subject of keeping leaves out of an ornamental pond is a difficult one. Mine is far too big to stretch a net over. This can be done with the smaller jobs. All I can do is to let the wind blow them near the bank and I can then rake them out, but they soon become sodden and sink. I don't suppose the carp will mind the leaves, they are such tough fish and can live in a few inches of water and, in a severe drought, can even sustain life in wet mud for a time.

As for the reservoirs in my part of the country they are almost as low as they were in the long dry summer we had a couple of years ago. A friend has offered to pump my big pool dry with one of his agricultural pumps this winter so I can get out all the sludge, but I am in two minds about the proposal. It means one pool will have to be filled again from local sources and my moorhen family would most certainly depart and I should be sad without them.

Whilst I was away wildfowling our caretaker took to feeding them three times a day, morning, midday and evening. Now the four of them wait around at these times, coming up to the french windows and peering in to remind me it is 'nosh' time. They seem to be getting on very well together and at the moment of writing they have not attempted to drive either of the two young away.

The Last Flight

My wildfowling week in January started ill for me as my back strain was plaguing me, so I missed a spectacular flight which Tom and the Doctor had on a high stubble not far from HQ. We had watched a build-up of greys for some days and the field was remote and not easy to view without powerful binoculars.

Apparently Tom and the Doc arrived at the field just before sunrise and found five other fowlers in the best places, armed with pump guns, and with decoys out. Whether or not they had permission to be there I do not know; each party challenged the other. So the Doc and Tom had to take the two lower positions.

I knew this particular ground well, as some three years ago I had shot on that very hill in a blinding snowstorm. A stone wall ran up the hill to a timber belt, with a steep bank which was sheer enough to give cover without a hide. It was one of those mornings when the greys are completely foolish, when not even shooting will turn them away.

The gang up the wall, apparently from all accounts, close together in a bunch, opened up a murderous fire on the incoming skeins. Tom told me he thought at least thirty-five or forty geese paid the penalty. Under such a barrage it is not surprising that the massacre was large, for each time the geese came in, two or three fell in a hail of lead. Tom and the Doc, being in the outlying position, only collected a goose apiece. Hearing their account made me glad I was not there on that morning, for the use of repeating guns is an abomination – no true wildfowler will own one.

Those flights I missed through my wretched back trouble were mostly uneventful, and I will only describe our last morning flight. Snow had whitened the high tops the night before and the dawn was clear of cloud and very cold with hardly any wind. We were on our chosen ground early; indeed, we had to wait in

7

the car before the first peep of dawn told us to be up and moving. There is always the chance of that early wandering goose in the dim half-light, geese which usually come without sound. I have an idea these are birds which have lost a mate, or maybe it is a loner seeking a gaggle for company.

We closed the car doors carefully so as not to wake the farmer and his wife and set off across the field. It was a long tramp. Ahead of me were the Doc and Tom, their forms barely visible in the half darkness, mere vague shapes which might be bushes or trees. I took up my position close to a fence in which grew quite tall trees, and over the fence was a deep burn in full flood which fretted and gurgled round a protruding root. There was a keening of plovers somewhere in the darkness and once, surprisingly, the 'cruik' of a moorhen. There was little need for a hide where I stood, for the grass on the burnside, bone coloured and dead, rose almost to my waist, and inter-mingled with it grew rusty stalks of sorrel and burdock.

To the east the sky was quickly paling as the earth rolled over. Soon I could see the silhouettes of trees etched against it, their edges 'burred' as in a drypoint etching. Soon there was goose talk afar off and intermittently. The skeins were restless and moving. Suddenly a dark shape, silent and with steady beat, passed wide on my left and in a moment was gone, one of those early customers which sometimes open proceedings. More goose talk! A curlew wailing, then silence again, and just the light growing. It was not unlike watching one of those 'instant' prints from a modern camera slowly taking shape, trees, hills, a water flash, growing more distinct.

I prefer the morning flight to the evening. When darkness closes down you know the thing is finished, no more chance of a shot. The growing light of dawn is full of promise and there is no stumbling walk back to the car. I had with me my game gun with which I had never shot a goose. I chose this as it was considerably less weight to carry and I am more used to it. In the right chamber I had a number three, in the left a number one. I heard, afar off the call of a greylag. It was coming my way.

One would have thought that, down the years, wild geese had learnt to be silent. Is there any other bird worthy of the gun who will announce to all and sundry he is coming? The cock pheasant, always a fool, advertises his bedroom for the night, mallards sometimes mutter among themselves as they fly, though it is a muted, cautious conversation. But the wild goose, whether it be grey, pink, or whitefront, announces his arrival in clarion tones. Very soon I spied my customer coming high across the now visible stubble. It never saw the silent figure with the pale labrador standing in the shadows.

The little gun swung up. At the shot the goose collapsed and fell not ten yards away on the edge of the burn. Polar slipped away and came back with it, delivering it right into my hand. Some minutes later a skein of seven greys came by, but I let them go for they were heading straight for Tom. I watched them swing up and right handed, one dropped, and soon after Doc had one down as well, across the burn.

So did our last flight end. And what better way than to get a goose with one's last shot? I was pleased, too, with my dog, who now knew what goose shooting was all about, and he had saved at least two greys from reaching the sideway. I must say that one's enjoyment is greatly enhanced by having a well-trained dog (an untrained one can be one hell of a nuisance, especially when flighting geese inland).

The sun was up when we reached the car. The busy world was about its business, tractors setting forth, all the work of the day began. And on that last morning, bacon and eggs seemed to go down with a greater enjoyment. There is nothing so hungry as a goosehunter after early morning flight!

Down to Earth

Last year a kind reader of my literary efforts arrived on my doorstep with a sack of the most marvellous potatoes, Désirée. This autumn, the potato-lifting period was almost over, and the twitch fires from the burning haulms ascended the soft grey skies, following on the stubble fires of September and late August and I almost gave up hope of further undeserved largesse, so much so that I purchased two bags of King Edwards from a neighbouring farm. I had hardly completed this transaction when I returned one day to find two half-hundredweight bags in my garage which had not been there when I went out. Yes! My faithful friend had again been generous. Such is the power of the pen!

And what potatoes they were! None of your big 'uns at the top layer and small 'pig' potatoes underneath, which is so often the case (unless the prospective buyer plunges the arm in deep). Every one would have graced a harvest festival layout; huge, perfect potatoes, as big as a baby's head, enough for two people and three meals. For a Désirée potato baked in its jacket, served up in a white clean napkin, scalding hot and steaming, with the addition of salt, black pepper, and knob of butter, is indeed a meal in itself, though not perhaps the diet for the weight watcher.

These gargantuan tubers can also be peeled, boiled for twenty minutes, and then cut up into knobs which are thereafter fried a golden russet in deep fat (making sure they are well salted before consigning to the boiling fat). These too are wonderful fare for a hungry man and you need little else to go with them unless it be two well-fried, rusky-dry bacon rashers. I have also tried a jacket Désirée with a knob of butter and dash of Worcestershire sauce within its burning heart – this is good, too, after tramping the winter fields with a gun.

One of the sacks contained Désirée, the other Pentland, a Scottish potato I suppose. Désirée has a rosy hue before being subjected to heat, a comforting glow such as one sees on the cheeks of old countrymen. Pentland is more a son of the soil, with an ordinary potato-colour outer skin, good enough on the table though I prefer the rosy one. King Edwards are of excellent flavour too, for I like a rather broken, floury flesh and not the soapy kind.

Richard Jefferies in one of his books, *Amaryllis At The Fair* describes the old farmer eating his potatoes 'Vorty vold' which he washed down with his home-brewed 'Goliath' ale. The description of the way the butter melts into the broken flesh of the tuber makes one's mouth water. It is Richard Jefferies at his best. His eye was so keen it missed nothing, and once read you never forget his description of how the old farmer's favourite fireside chair and oak panelling was worn through years and years of sitting, of the wearing away of the fibres of the wood, just as the feet of pilgrims wear away the stone steps to a shrine.

When Richard Jefferies wrote those words he was poor and almost a dying man and could eat little. One can sense a certain wistful longing in his description of the old man's enjoyment of his food. Most of the farming community enjoy their 'vitulls', as well they might, always working in the open air, a fine healthy life indeed and a natural one – the envy, I am sure, of many a factory worker or coal miner. I look for the day when men need no longer grub like moles in the darkness of the earth, shut a way from this glorious world (which could be even more delectable if we only watched our step). Man was never meant to toil in the bowels of the earth; to my mind no wealth can ever recompense those who have to win a living at the coal face. This time is coming very soon; atomic power will make it unnecessary, if only we can get our priorities right, and keep iron hands on this potentially deadly discovery.

Sadly, in the hard frosty and snowy weather around Christmastime my moorhens departed I know not where, though they showed up at intervals to share their morning feed with a multitude of starlings. But long before dark they were gone. I could not guess where they went to roost. I have a thick planting of conifers all down my outside fence, they may sleep there, or again there is an ivy-clad apple tree, a venerable tree which provides us each year with small, old-fashioned cooking apples, bad keepers but delicious in a pie.

I planted the ivy there myself when I first bought the property. In the space of a dozen years it has raced up, smothering the branches. The old tree now wears a thick winter overcoat in which other birds love to sleep – the sparrows, wrens, and finches.

The ivy produces many berries. To them the fat woodpigeons used to come in the hard weather, clumsily shaking the thick leaves until the snow fell in little avalanches and gulping down the berries like greedy boys gobble sweets. But we have few woodpigeons now in my part of the country, and when the flocks do come they do not stay more than a day or so and then pass on. The recognised roosting woods are empty, as they were last winter.

I love to walk in the forest when the snow lies white. You can see a long way between the hardwoods now the leaves are down and mysterious undiscovered alleyways and clearings are revealed. Everywhere are the footprints of the wild creatures of the woods, the tiny fairy-like lacing of mice, the single-track spoor of foxes, the 'sturdy-toes' spoor of the badger, the cloven marks of delicate-footed deer. Rabbit tracks loop about the bramble thickets, the three-toed marks of pheasants are there plain to see, and many a midnight kill can be traced: rose-pink blood marks soaked into the snow, and feathers, and the fox's 'pounce' can be read by those with eyes to see.

Again and again on my woodland walks I see the black and white pictures which I can later transfer to my drawing board for I have always been an admirer of black and white, almost in preference to colour. In dead winter the sky is bruised ochre, the snow so white in contrast to the delicate filigree of bare black twigs, and sturdy trunks of oak and ash. See how the ash branches curve over and sweep upwards at the tips like some of the hairstyles that women adopt, see in contrast the wriggly higgledy-piggledy oak boughs and twigs which never seem to know where they are going. Then look at the graceful beech trees whose branches, like those of the ash, tend to sweep downwards in graceful curves. The tall ash poles swing and rock like no other woodland tree, they swing in the winter wind as though they had heavy weights on their tips and the trunks seem to take a long time to taper off. In the cold winter dusk when the snow lies blurred in the half light they rock uneasily and make a faint, dry clatter. Sometimes where one branch bears upon another they creak and wheeze as though they were something more than trees.

I like to be there in the gathering winter gloom to listen to the talk of the forest, there is something there which appeals to the primitive man, the hunter maybe, walking soft-footed through the woods intent on winning his next meal. The old tawnies are vociferous on these snowy nights calling one to another down the dark aisles; maybe too you can hear the bark of a fox as he sets out on his evening hunt with perhaps the vision of a nice trim vixen somewhere around.

The North Wind

On the very top of my roof there is a weathervane of my own design, cunningly wrought for me by a local ironmaster. Needless to say this weathervane is in the shape of a greylag goose with neck astrain and wings raised so that his beak always cleaves the wind. It is (at the time of writing) the only one in the village which is visible to the wayfarer. I often see the rustics cock an eye as they pass by on the road to see which way the wind blows. (The townsman takes little notice of the weather, it means nothing to him, why should it? Most of his working life is spent under cover.)

The other night, in a frozen and forbidding dusk, I looked up to see the old bird with his beak to the north and before I went to bed small rustling flakes had started to fall, mantling the ice on my big pond, where, in the faraway heats of summer, my moorhen family reared their two broods. Sure enough, when I awoke next morning, along with my daughter, dogs, and garden birds, the earth was white. Even the old goose was white and the sky was the colour of putty.

At noon it seemed like late afternoon. The snow fell steadily all day, traffic crawled, spewing slush in filthy bow waves, and the thrushes hopped miserably about the lawn, trying to find the last of the apple fallings which I had left for them. Certainly it was an afternoon for a walk in the forest. I would take my .22 rifle and the labrador. The rifle is more akin to the bow and arrow, therefore it pleases me. There is no scatter of shot, just the one crumb of lead which must fly true.

Over the forest the sky was menacing; trees seem to gather dark vapours (fog is always more dense in a wood), and against the black firs multitudes of white flakes flew diagonally. I find woodland in snow quite enchanting; there is mystery everywhere, along the ridings, up the narrow alleyways of the firs, where, even there, in those sheltered aisles, the snow had found

14

its way. As I walked along the path I thought of a day last July when I passed along this very track, how the heat was almost unsupportable and I wore no coat or shirt. What a change it now was! A different country entirely.

I passed up the narrow track to where it joined the main riding. The snow fell ever more thickly. Standing at the junction of a path I listened. There was only the soft rustle of the flakes and now and again the faint sigh of the wind in the firs. At any time conifers are dark and lacking in bird life, save for goldcrests and the nefarious jays and magpies. I remembered that somewhere here the long-eared owls have nested, noble owls indeed, more regal, and far less common, than the tawny. And a little way on among new plantings the nightjar churrs in the scented twilights of June.

In the snow were the prints of fallow deer and the little hunch-backed Japanese deer which somehow found their way here from Woburn, many miles to the south. Strange little misshapen creatures rarely seen and, I believe, extremely good to eat. And here let me say, since we talk of appetites, what better afternoon to stalk the woodland rabbits, or even a hare, for there are a number in the forest? It is the hunter's hour.

In any other year the woodpigeon would be coming in, seeking out the warm firs this winter night, but of late they and the collared dove also have become much less plentiful, so much so I suspect some poisoning is going on and the powers that be are keeping it dark.

I left the firs and was soon among the hardwoods. It was surprising to find so much leaf on the oaks and the beeches too. Everywhere the tracks of rabbits were laced about and other lesser spoors of mice and little birds. I stepped back under a solitary stunted fir which grew beside the ride. Beneath was a mere dusting of snow and the dark tasselled boughs above my head were thick and dark, forming a cosy thatch. Against the grey sky three woodpigeon arrowed over, making for the

firs. Something moved at the far end of the ride. My glasses were focused in a moment. It was a fallow buck. He appeared intensely black against the white background and for quite two minutes he stood staring down the ride towards me. Then he slowly walked across and vanished in the dense cover.

The deer here seek out the thickest and most remote part of the woods in which to lie up during the day, choosing those places where the blackthorn grows and the undercover is thick. They shun the fir forest, though I have seen the little humpbacks there. When the buck had gone a great loneliness seemed to fall about me, nothing but the ceaseless snow and the hardly heard rustle and caress of the flakes. No bird flew against that sombre sky, no rabbit moved against the white snow.

Quickly the dusk came down on the wintry wilderness. By the time I reached the road the lights of the village were like stars through the snow. Looking upwards, I said goodnight to my goose weathercock. His beak was still cleaving the north wind. Then I went in to muffins and a blazing fire of apple-wood.

The Last 'Cocks Only'

When, during the last few days of January, I heard that the keeper's wife had found her false teeth embedded in ice over night (resembling those prehistoric insects which have been found embedded in amber) I knew that this winter was becoming pretty rough. I awoke on the 26th to find all the outside pipes frozen, and there was a sullen lake in the bottom of the bath which refused to gurgle away. I have no truck with blow lamps. I wrap rags round the pipes and set them alight with the help of paraffin. Then I sit down and await that discreet gurgle and the subsequent rush of water down the plug hole. This system of unfreezing pipes is better than calling the plumber or fiddling around with blow lamps which snuff out in the slightest breeze. But don't make the fire too big or you may have to call the fire brigade. This method is not recommended for wooden bungalows or lath-and-plaster Essex walls. But never fear, I am not going to talk about the weather, though it must be admitted that a covering of snow *does* simplify a landscape in rather a charming way. Trees are plain silhouettes, so are hedges and woods; there is no such thing as a 'complicated' landscape when snow covers the ground.

I had a go at the cocks on the last Saturday afternoon in January. It was a day of brilliant sun and blinding glare from the snow which made one's eyes ache, and one really needed sunglasses. From Bob's kale there arose a mighty concourse of pigeon. Some even sat hunched on the kale tops until we were well in range, but we did not shoot for we were after the wily old cocks which harbour in the lane close by. I took station by a gently steaming muck heap which no doubt the poor black-birds, thrushes and tits found comforting in the terrible cold; indeed their delicate footprints were all over the snow, as were the prints of partridge and pheasant. Fred Johnson was in the lane, the Doctor along the side of the straggling trees, and Charlie, Bob's 'orraman' and Bob himself drove the lane towards us. Two cocks went out of the kale, saluted by Charlie without visible damage, and a few hens came rocketing out and a swerving blackbird or two. That was that. We then went down into the valley to the artichoke belt, planted for the express purpose of harbouring pheasants. I wonder more shooting men do not make refuges out of artichokes, the cover lasts for years and if you want an artichoke for the table there you are!

I stood in the snow on the east side of the cover, the other guns were out of sight of me on the far end. I saw Bob and Charlie beating out a boundary and Bob's retrievers and spaniels diving in and out of the thickset hedge. Charlie went across the snowy field. I saw hares getting up and running. He shot one before it reached the artichokes. I expected a cock to come my way but only hens came whirring overhead with quivering tails. After the drive was over I found I had Fred's Purdey, and he had my AYA; we had unwittingly changed weapons in the Land-Rover when we piled in with the dogs. A tight fit it was, too. I felt I was at the bottom of a rugger scrum. When the tail board went down we all fell out in a heap.

After this abortive drive, we then again crammed into the Land-Rover, dogs and all. How the dogs enjoy this intimacy with their masters! Steaming coats, panting tongues and clambering, oblivious of curses; a real man's outing this and no mistake. I must say I found the warmth of about six dogs' bodies was not unwelcome on that freezing afternoon.

We next debouched around Bob's fir spinney where surely there must be a cock or two. I was in my favourite spot down by the brook facing the firs. Fred was up on my left and two other guns over the stream to guard the southern boundary. For a while, utter silence, that silence which is always so puzzling to the waiting guns. Whatever can the beaters be doing? The sky is already showing signs of the day's end, a huge red sun is burning down behind the dead elms by Fred Allen's farm. It's an intriguing farm, for it has a walled garden and an old monastic pond close by which I persuaded Fred to stock with carp. Though the pond is shallow these carp have grown hugely and double figures are not uncommon. At one end is a reed-mace bed and a pheasant often harbours there – but we haven't reached the farm yet, let us concentrate on the matter in hand, i.e. the fir wood.

A startled blackbird came swerving out of the firs followed by a pigeon. There was a distant shot but it sounded very far away. Something was moving down by the brook, and I saw it was a rabbit. It came out of the hedge and sat in the snow looking very miserable, rolled up like a ball. I wondered if it was a 'mixy'. Far off, a shout. A cock came out of the firs, tail streaming behind, It offered a shot which I like above all others, passing high and to the right. It crumpled and hit the snow and I sent Polar for it before anyone else loosed his dog. It does annoy me when another dog is sent for my bird, which so often happens in a rough shoot. When I get a bird down, whether it is a goose or a pheasant, I like my own dog to retrieve it at once. A cock went past Fred on the hill but it was a long shot – we saw it go back to the shelter of the kale we had 'beat out' at the beginning of the afternoon. Then I saw a cock come out of the firs, run along the fence, and dodge back in again.

The beaters were getting closer now. A shot or two rang out and several hens came out; some over Fred, some over me. Then another cock coming straight for me, an easy shot! I swung the gun up. I had two shots at him and missed with both; he, too, went back to the kale. What had I done wrong? Perhaps it was too easy! I don't like a bird coming straight over me. I cannot quite remember how we finished up at the fir wood. I think Bob had had one on the way up, I know the Doctor missed one. We went on, now to Fred Allen's farm. I went over a plank bridge some fifty yards or more from the reedy carp pond. A snipe flickered along the brook and went into the snow-clad bushes opposite the Doctor. I thought at the time it was a woodcock. I only had a fleeting glimpse. Fred and his spaniels came up to the pond and a cock pheasant burst out of the reeds coming straight for me, a shot which was exactly like my last one. This time the gun seemed to come up more easily. I blotted out the cock and squeezed the trigger. The pheasant fell in the stream to be retrieved by Fred's black labrador before I could loose Polar.

What the total bag was I cannot quite be sure, something in the region of eight or nine pheasants, and a hare. A paltry enough bag by most standards but how much more enjoyable than a great slaughter! The brilliant day, the crisp snow, the cold clear blue sky, it was just the sort of day I enjoy with the gun and I had had a pheasant with my very last shot of the game season, something I always like to do.

A few days later I went with daughter Angela to see if there were any interesting fowl on Blatherwyck Lake near Oundle, a very lovely sheet of water surrounded by fine trees. We stopped by the low wall and got out the glasses. The lake was partly frozen, but at the western end near the farm there was a wide space of open water and a long ice sheet on which stood and sat some thirty greylags, real wild visitors, one small barnacle goose, and a magnificent snow goose, not an albino grey or pink, but a genuine snow goose with black flight feathers, one of the few snow geese I have ever seen in the wild. Once it stood and flapped its wings, a most handsome goose with a smaller bill than the heavy orange mandibles of the grey. Beyond the ice floe there were mallard and Canadas and five goosanders together with pochard and mallard. Most of the greys, including the snow goose, soon settled down to sleep, though one old grey had his head up and called frequently, that lovely sound I had not heard since last November. What a pleasure it was to see my old friends sitting on that midland pool so far from their usual haunts, secure now for another six months at least! There was a grebe not far off which looked to me very like a Slavonian grebe. Altogether it was a brave show of wildfowl.

21

Memories Stirred

Two things caught my eye in a recent issue of the *Shooting Times* and both brought back memories. One was Geoffrey Boothroyd's article on the 'New Service' Colt revolver. To my great chagrin I was obliged to surrender mine after the last war as the police would not let me retain it. It was a new weapon and with it I almost won the battalion revolver competition. I was beaten by a fellow officer who, rather unfairly, fought out the final with a special target pistol of his own. That rankled a good deal for I maintained that all the weapons should have been the same army pattern. After the war I advertised mine for sale but received no offers. I often wondered what became of it for it was in mint condition. I suppose it was dumped in the sea, along with thousands of other rifles and pistols.

The other subject was Fred Taylors' article on the Nith Hotel on the Solway. Long before the war I used to go there in January during the Bill Powell era, though I never went out with him, preferring to work mostly on my own. There was, however, another fisherman/fowler in the village who went with me sometimes. For the life of me I cannot remember his surname, though his Christian name was Robert. He was a big man and a grand type, a good shot, too. I remember one moonlight night when we were out on the marshes opposite Carlaverock Castle. We were after the barnacles, then of course unprotected. We had to cross one of the wide gutters where the sand was horribly 'quick' in the middle. Robert went over first and nearly got stuck, I followed. Being lighter I made the passage without undue trouble but the thought lay in the back of my mind that we would have to return across that gutter before the tide turned.

Robert went on towards Stanhope, I elected to sit in a shallow gutter to await events. I could hear the barnacles on the move yelping like a pack of Pekinese puppies, quite a different cry to that of the pinks or greys. The big packs seemed to be moving around in the moonlight. It wasn't long before I heard two shots far away to the east. Those were the days when few people ever shot on the Solway.

I know Robert was 'having a go' and awaited his return with some interest, though it was by no means a good night for shooting as the moon was full, shining clear and hard from a frosty sky. Whilst I sat cogitating on the still and frozen scene, with the water gleaming like a bright spear under Criffel, I was suddenly aware of the faint croak of geese. Out from the land came six greylags barely tree-top height. They came smack over my head and I never touched a bird, possibly because I was using my old single 8-bore Belching Bess.

It was one of the worst misses I can remember, only matched by just such another occasion, again on a moonlight night, on another estuary when I had a big skein of pinks slap over my head not a gunshot high.

I suppose it must have been about three in the morning before I heard Robert returning. In his bag were two beautiful barnacles, but he was covered in mud from the neck downwards and this was already freezing on him. Apparently he had got into a quicksand and he had to 'roll out' as he termed it. I remember looking with great envy at his barnacles for I had up to that time never shot one, and though he tried to give me one of his, I rightly refused.

One year I went with a friend who had a very good labrador which was an excellent goose dog, strong enough to tackle any tide. It slept in the gunroom. Next morning when we came down to breakfast we found it had pulled down the curtains and had eaten part of them. I knew then why the dog had not been left in the car.

Some dogs have this woeful failing. One of mine ruined a car seat and chewed up a whole packet of cigarettes as well as a half-pound block of chocolate. He threw up the whole mess inside

my car for good measure. I know one man who foolishly left his
dog in the back of his Rolls. When he returned the back seat was
in rags and the stuffing all over the floor. It was a new Rolls, too,
a make of car that few of my shooting buddies aspire to.

Then, as now, there was a lot of hard drinking by the
Glencapel fowlers. Though I enjoy my pint as much as the next
man, drinking to excess always seemed to me to be both futile,
expensive, and acutely uncomfortable afterwards. A man who
accompanied me one year was hardly ever capable of going out
to flight and I had to soldier on my own, which I preferred
anyway, for the true wildfowler is a loner, his activities are more
akin to that of a sniper in wartime, lying up, well concealed, and
awaiting the right moment.

One of my old fowling comrades of those days had indeed
been a sniper in World War One, Howard Seth Smith who, I
am delighted to say, is still very active and as keen as ever on
shooting. Howard was as tough as they come and would sit out
all day on the marshes or in the reed beds like an old fox waiting
for his prey. Though he had been gravely wounded in the arm
and hand in the war he was a good shot and had a special way of
mounting his gun.

I saw a short while ago a reference to dogs revelling in snow.
Even our Pekinese delights in it and goes completely mad, though
I must say that the great snows of the first part of February were
too engulfing for his small frame; indeed he got firmly stuck in
a drift, and could not move until my daughter rescued him.

But old Polar, my labrador, had a whale of a time, racing
about, bounding in and out of the drifts, his silly old grinning
face a mask of white. I wonder why it is that dogs have such a
love of snow, I suppose they are like children in this respect. I
must confess that it has always had an attraction for me, too, that
glittering white mantle which looks so like icing sugar.

Just before the big snow I paid a visit to the Eye Brook reservoir, a very favourite summer fishing haunt of mine where

everything is beautifully arranged and sited for the angler. You can take your car right down to the boats, there is a cosy 'chat' room and offices within a few yards, and courteous people to attend to your wants. It presented a very different picture in the hard spell, for it was frozen over from bank to bank with only very few leads of open water for the wildfowl.

Many had departed, but at the northern end, where the water is shallow, there was a great company of wigeon and Canada geese all busily feeding on the grass verges by the little bridge. There was only a powdering of snow on the grass where the wind had blown away deeper drifts and among the Canadas I spied four beautiful snow geese. I had previously seen one single snow goose at Blatherwycke but here were four of these lovely birds! Through my Zeiss I could bring them within touching distance and could see there were no rings on their legs. Like the goose I saw at Blatherwycke one would raise itself up and flap its wings, showing the jet-black flight feathers which make such a wonderful contrast to the snow-white plumage.

The little wigeon were burrowing about in the grass like moles and sometimes were barely visible. The cock wigeon is surely one of the prettiest of our ducks, though it must be admitted that our old friend the drake mallard is a mighty fine fellow when in the pink of condition, with that jutting chestnut breast which is perhaps nearer to a madder red in colour, shot with glancing blue lights, that brilliant gleaming emerald head and neck, and the orange legs and white tail feathers which overhang the almost black under-tail coverts. And what a jaunty touch is that impertinent curl in his tail feathers! He always gives the impression of being rather a pompous character, but the shape of his bill belies this for it is set in a permanent smirk.

Amid the Tangled Thorns

During the exceptionally severe weather we had at the beginning of February I found it difficult to keep pace with the demands of what the Victorians called 'our feathered friends'. Just outside my french windows I placed the bird table, and from it I suspended 'Christmas stockings' of mixed nuts, large lumps of suet, and the sad relics of the Christmas turkey.

The latter was at first regarded with some suspicion until a bold tit (a great tit of course) dared to fly in and perch on the keel bone. Then the scrum started with a vengeance. Hordes of starlings arrived from nowhere, like vultures on a dead zebra. It's amazing how starlings will soon gather at any food that is going; one moment there is not one in sight, the next you have a black mass, resembling a horde of shiny beetles, all squabbling and fighting over the food. The majority of our wintering starlings are foreigners, indeed, there is a great decline in the numbers of our home-bred birds. A pair comes every April to breed in the hole in one of my old apple trees on the lawn. Horrific battles take place at that time, rival pairs become locked together, for, like moorhens, a fighting starling turns on its back and strikes out with its claws. At these times you may almost pick them up, for they fight with great ferocity oblivious of any danger.

Every evening at this time of the year just before they migrate, I see the big flocks passing over to some distant roost, some secluded thorny wilderness, for the starling does not usually roost in firs. They prefer a tangled wood where the bare old thorns are massed together, or larch woods.

Their other favourite roosts are, of course, in the centres of our big cities. I remember when I did a series of late-night nature talks for the BBC in Birmingham I often stood in amazement to see and hear the thousands of starlings roosting on the ledges and cornices of the principal buildings near the Bullring. They like the warmth and bustle; indeed their own nightly concert

could often be heard above the roar of the traffic. Yet towards midnight all fell asleep and one could see the round puffed-out balls of the silent sleeping birds on the ledges. As far as I am aware the starling is the only bird which *will* flock into the cities for sleep. I suppose it is warmer there, and as it is an essentially gregarious bird it finds the noise, bustle and bright lights greatly to its taste. Strange then that out in the wild countryside, where the nights are silent, cold and still, where there are no warm lights or bustling traffic, they should seek out the thorny, lonely covers, many of which abound in the Pytchley country, which were planted as harbours for Charles James.

I once had the shooting of such a fox cover. There were a few oaks and black poplars at one end but the rest of the wood was almost impenetrable thorn and sloe with no wide ridings at all, only well-trodden runways of badger, fox and rabbit, which wound about. The whole of the woodland floor was clothed in green moss for it was a very damp spot and nothing else would grow there. Like the badger and fox I used to creep along these private runways with my gun, and I sometimes managed to bag the odd pheasant, though it was mostly pigeons and rabbits that I was after. The former flocked to the cover, which was in a fold of the fields, well sheltered from the north wind. As evening fell, and the owls began to hoot, I would hear and see the starling flocks wheeling about overhead in a sort of tribal dance which went on until sundown, when one by one the black birds would drop down like stones into the tall straggling thorns above me and there continue their deafening chatter for a while.

Our home-bred birds feed on wire worms, their favourite diet in spring, and as the pastures are now drenched with sprays the starlings pick up the dead worms and perish, or, if they get a mild dose, the eggs are infertile. Now some ten years ago, or perhaps a little longer, before these sprays were in general use, the starling flocks, all young birds, were a feature of the Midland meadows in June where their 'churring' cries sounded from every buttercup field. For the last five years my garden starlings have failed to rear young. Eggs are laid, sometimes there is a feeble hunger cry from a youngster, but then all is silent. If the nesting hole is examined the half-fledged young can be seen lying dead inside. I do not know if this is the case all over the country, I can only speak for my Midland area where agriculture is intense.

A few chaffinches came for the wild bird seed I put out in the February snows, cocks and hens mixed. We never see now the great flocks of males and females, always separate, which were a feature of the days before the agricultural sprays. It is a 'bachelor finch' no longer, for that was the old country name of the chaffinch because of the habit of the males banding together in the winter months.

To return, in memory, to those winter evening expeditions of mine to that remote fox cover: there was but one narrow ride through the place and that was for the convenience of the hunt when they drew the cover (which very rarely failed to show a fox) and the hunting paths I followed were never marked by any human spoor save my own, and no wonder, for at times I had to crawl on all fours to get along them!

I liked to think of all the woodland people who were somewhere all around me as I crept about those hunting paths: the mice under the moss and, in the old ash-stump roots which were full of holes and hollows like fairy caves, the hibernating hedgehogs, tucked up warm and snug, the grey squirrels up in the few straggly oaks where their dreys were visible (I shot those pests often and relished their white meat); the badgers, deep in their sett hearing me moving overhead, no doubt grumbling at the intrusion of their kingdom, the wily red fox with his nose in his brush and one ear flicking and cocking when he heard me.

Once, as I crept from one of my hunting paths into a small clearing I surprised a woodcock as it rocketed up against a saffron sunset sky, I dropped him in a cloud of feathers and my dog brought him back.

The pheasants were wily; I rarely bagged one, for the cover was so dense it was impossible to get a clear shot, The only intimation of an old cock was a sudden explosion among the thorns and a brief glimpse of a long tail departing. One shot at a pheasant remains in my mind. I was nearing the edge of the cover by a hunting gate when a cock pheasant jumped from a drainage gutter. I took a snap shot as it went through the tangled thorns and heard it drop. I also heard the dying batter of its wings, then silence. Now a pheasant was regarded as a real prize and I plunged into the thickets (I had no dog with me that day), but though I searched as well as I could, even squirming on my stomach under the sharp thorns, I could not locate that bird. Dusk was falling and I became almost bushed in the dense cover. I think it must have lodged up in the branches; I never found it, and so sharp was my disappointment I remember the incident to this day.

Yet what fun those times were! True days of a lone hunter, something quite apart from a set shooting party, and infinitely more enjoyable.

Whoopers over Godolphin

We seem to have been seeing the caption 'bleak winds' on our goggle screens fairly often this winter and my garden pool has been locked in ice for weeks. Some days the ice partially melts but leaves a film of water on the surface.

With the last 'cocks only' day behind me there is nothing left to shoot but rabbits, hares, and pigeon. In my dreary 'Midland plain' we have scarcely any pigeon at all this winter, and even the collared doves seem to be becoming scarce. Can it be that the days of the great pigeon flocks are over, when one saw whole fields blue with them? The farmer welcomes their departure, as he did the going of the rabbit, though now the latter has staged a come-back. From a purely selfish viewpoint I hope the pigeon do come back before winter's end as I delight in waiting in the woods in the long March twilights.

The other afternoon, having the urge upon me, I decided to visit Godolphin Pond again. So I took the 12-bore and with my labrador set off up the old drove road. On one side of this ancient parkway grow numerous oaks. Nearly every one was thick with ivy. One tree, quite a large one, had been completely enveloped, the ivy growing out even to the tips of the branches so that the tree resembled a huge leafy ball.

Usually at this time of year, when we are nearing the end of winter, I am always sure of a shot or two at the pigeon who resort to the oaks for the ivy berries, just as it is a sure find for acorning pheasants when the leaves are down. But on that recent afternoon no pigeon were to be seen. The withered weeds along the ditches were white with frost, puddles in the lane itself were roofed with white 'cats' ice', which broke underfoot with a noise of clinking glass, and it was indeed a bleak and biting wind which rattled in the shining dark green ivy leaves.

There was a dank mist lying over the winter-bitten fields and the only two birds I saw up the old drove road were a robin and a cock blackbird who was throwing the frozen leaves about in the ditch in a hopeless fashion. He was puffed and feeble and did not fly away as we passed. Once away from the drove road on the rising ground the snow lay in ribs, and where the drifts met the laid branches of the starved hedges it had blown through the apertures protruding out into the stubble in rounded bolsters of hard frozen snow.

Soon I could see the trees around Godolphin Pond and the bare wriggly branches of the oaks. For how many years had they defied the bleak winds, two generations of men, three? Maybe more!

As I walked up the furrow, my boots scrunching on the ribs of snow, a great russet and grey hare started up, seeming to appear like some magician's trick, for the stubble was so short it could barely hide a lark. Her ears were laid flat, the powerful back legs spurred her on, and when she was some sixty yards distant the large black tipped ears were erected and her speed dropped to that easy, deceptively slow, canter.

I had a hare hanging in the larder at home so she went unscathed. Polar the labrador, who had leapt to the end of his tether, slunk back to heel. He was never properly trained, and it takes a good animal to be free from chase.

It was difficult to approach in silence because of the crunching snow. One step at a time and then the pond bobbed into view. Alas! There was no open water. It was a spotless white sheet of ice, strong enough to bear my weight. I walked across, at first with caution, and then with growing confidence. The tracks of moorhens and pheasants criss-crossed in all directions, as did the tiny prints of birds, rats and mice. What secret trafficking goes on at night! One could read the white surface like the page of a book.

Round one of the locked-fast willow stems were black rabbit currants and the bark had been stripped upwards by about a foot. The rabbit (or hare) must have stood up on its back pads to reach so high.

I stood there watching and listening. Westwards the sun was huge and red, magnified to frightening proportions by the mist. Then I heard a wonderful sound not heard since I sat by my campfire one autumn night up far Glengarry, the strange unearthly cry of whooper swans. A string of seven passed across the sunset, bound no doubt for that vast and beautiful expanse of water which rivals Lake Windermere - Empingham reservoir to the north, surely to be the most impressive expanse of water anywhere in the Midlands, or indeed in England. I saw the construction of this enormous lake from its very beginnings, and have watched the shining water creeping up in stealthy fashion along its varied creeks and valleys.

There should be royal fishing there when it is finally stocked but it is so vast I should think it will be difficult to locate the trout. Perhaps, who knows, we may get the whitefronts coming back to our part of the country, as they did near Oundle at the beginning of the century, if they have so vast a sanctuary?

I watched those Hans Andersen birds fade into the white mists and turned for home. My bag was empty but what matter?

This winter landscape, now fast fading in the dusk, seemed as empty as a Canadian wilderness, yet despite this, there was, I fancied, a subtle smell in the air, a sharp sweetness. This, coupled with the lengthening twilight, made me think of coming spring.

The Ancient Fear

At around six-thirty the other morning my daughter awoke me with the news that a heron was on the pond. He is a rogue which has been clearing up all the goldfish ponds in the neighbourhood and I saw on my lawn one large 2 lb goldfish with a stab wound, a fish I have had for over ten years. The trouble with a rogue heron is that he will come again and again until he has cleared a pond, and he will come under the moon, or in the early morning, just when it is getting light. I let off a blank cartridge and he flapped away over the boundary hedge. Ever since, I have kept a storm lantern burning on the lawn each night.

Herons are expert poachers. Last year an owner of a trout farm told me that if there was the smallest hole in the netting a heron would find its way through; they are a pest on trout farms. What struck me was how the fish in my pond were shocked into immobility. Usually they cruise about in full view, and come to be fed, including two magnificent golden orfe which must weigh close on 3 lbs and which I have had for fifteen years. Looking at the water you would not have guessed there was a fish in the pond and for two days they remained hidden in the mud and weeds. This shows what I call the 'Ancient Fear'. Man is not feared like the predators of the wild because we appeared on earth long after the birds of prey and the heron.

At my old home we had a large outdoor aviary in the grounds which contained a pair of hawfinches and other birds. It was planted up with thick bushes and they bred there. One day when I was looking out of the window a sparrowhawk made a swoop at the wire. The birds scattered in panic and for quite an hour afterwards they remained like little stuffed dummies, perched in the bushes, eyes wide in a sort of hypnotic trance. When

34

sparrowhawks were common I often witnessed the same thing when one made a swoop at finches. They rushed into the hedge, and one could almost pick them off the branches.

Even man has something of the 'Ancient Fear' when a sudden sound, a breaking stick, or even a pheasant bursting from underfoot like a bomb, can make the heart jump if one is alone in the wilds.

We have enormous fun with our moorhen family. The parents stayed with us all through the winter, only leaving when the pond was frozen over. When the ice covers the pool they are vulnerable, for foxes prey on them. They then roost in hedges and trees like pheasants, for the water is no longer a protection. Foxes dislike swimming, and vermin, like stoats and cats, will not enter water if they can help it.

The most feared of all winged predators are, of course, the peregrine and sparrowhawk. I was once waiting in a wood for pigeon and was startled when literally, out of the blue, there fell into the wood, and I mean fell, some twenty or forty pigeon. They came through the upper branches like stones and I glimpsed a peregrine sweep overhead. This was a wonderful example of the ancient fear, for even when the pigeon saw me down on the wood floor, they were loth to take wing; like the hunted finches and sparrows they seemed to be carved in stone.

I remember, too, standing beside a haystack sheltering from a shower. All at once numbers of sparrows, cheeping with frantic fear, descended all round me, and a sparrowhawk came sweeping round the angle of the stack and snatched a sparrow close beside me.

Likewise, fish in a pool seem to know instinctively when an otter is about. At my old home, where we had a lake stocked with trout and carp, if there was an otter about, the pool went dead, and not a fish was to be seen. Even worms, hunted by their ancient enemy the mole, can often be seen surfacing, though, like a rabbit pursued by a stoat, they have little chance of escape.

The fisherman, requiring worms, knows that to stick a fork in the ground and to work it to and fro will often persuade worms to surface, for they think a mole is active.

Man may be feared by wild creatures, but this fear is nothing compared with the 'ancient fear' which goes back such a long way into the dim past.

Hedgerow Homes

The other day, when on a country walk, I devised an amusing game, 'old' nest spotting. In the tall hawthorn hedges which so far have escaped the attention of the mechanical cutters it was an interesting test of bird knowledge akin to bird-watching.

The tiny buds of spring were just beginning to show as pale points and looking along the side of the hedges I could see that pinkish bloom which showed the sap was rising.

First and most conspicuous were the nests of blackbirds and thrushes, both mud-cupped but, in the case of the blackbirds, lined with dead grass. Some were tilted, and many on closer inspection revealed they had been adapted by mice as storehouses for berries.

Having such a durable mud-cement lining, these nests withstand the winter well. Then, as I walked along, I came upon a sparrow colony, ten bundles of untidy dead-grass balls. The house sparrows, when hedgerow nesting, always form a colony for they are sociable creatures. Very vulgar and ill-mannered they are too, as can be witnessed many a time in the garden where they indulge in sudden fierce 'demos', fighting, biting, and making a lot of noise, the only birds which do this outside the breeding season. Incidentally these vulgar street brawls always centre on one female who perhaps has a more powerful attraction for the opposite sex than her sisters, but once started, everyone joins in. I have sometimes actually caught two struggling males, little balls of fury with bills interlocked.

Then I came upon the nests of greenfinch and hedge sparrow. You might say, how can these nests be identified? The answer is – by observation. The nest of the greenfinch is sturdily built with moss and twigs and is of considerable size, that of the hedge sparrow smaller and with less moss, and lower in the hedge bottom.

Then, unmistakably, here and there, was the frail root basket of the bullfinch, quite a distinctive nest and not to be confused with that of any other British finch. On close examination one can see the fine root lining and the outer framework of little twigs, about three to four inches long. It is even possible to see if the young have hatched, and most likely flown, from traces of 'scurf' in the lining and one or two dried white droppings on the rim. Yet the young of the bullfinch are cleanly little creatures, always evacuating over the edge of the nest even when small, and the parents are particular to carry away the droppings as soon as they are evacuated. They wait on the nest rim after feeding to catch the droppings.

Soon I saw the nest of a goldfinch, right at the tip of a thorn spray, high in the hedge. From a distance it looked the size of a 12-bore 'mop' we use for gun cleaning, perhaps a trifle larger. On examining these old goldfinch nests you can often see a crust of dried droppings all round the rim, for they are not too keen on sanitation, but many nests remain as they were built which shows the young did not hatch. Lower in the hedges, where dead 'gix' stalks intermingle with the briars, you can see the frail hay cups of blackcaps, whitethroats and garden warblers.

On this particular walk I came upon a new nest, almost completed, of a longtailed tit. These little birds are early breeders and nearly always build their first nests before the leaves have come and consequently fall victim to marauding jays and magpies, to say nothing of boys (if indeed boys still go nest hunting). These nests are exquisitely made, lichen 'vanity' bags, elastic and wonderfully woven. They have to be elastic because the young are numerous, different from most other small birds which have only four or five young.

This old hawthorn hedge which I am describing has not been laid for some twenty years but when I reached the end of it I found my old friend John had begun operations. Soon that dormitory will be no more, at least for a while, but how much better to see a well-laid hedge such as this than a horrible row of bare slashed sticks with the tops cut off which now seems to be the modern craze. Hedge-laying in the Midlands is fast dying out. What a pity that is!

The flat platform of a woodpigeon's nest is another familiar feature of the old tall hawthorn hedges. In the more remote pastures the magpie chooses the thorns for his large fortified dome of sticks, built by a rogue with a guilty conscience, for the magpie is a great robber of other people's houses, though I cannot imagine any other British bird bold enough to tackle a magpie's nest and young. The only entrance is guarded by the pickaxe bill of the brooding hen; it is a postern door to her castle.

At one time it was possible to see the old nests of the now rare and shy hawfinch, built always on a horizontal bough of an orchard tree, such as I saw many years ago in Worcestershire, which county was a stronghold of this lovely handsome finch.

I noticed at the end of the lane that the rooks were active; the familiar nesting 'caw' is one of the most pleasing sounds of the English spring. Many nests were built in the elm tops but those trees which had been killed by elm disease were shunned, rightly so. A dead tree will not give to the wind; the nests would soon be sent flying in the first big gale. The live elm tops 'give' like a fishing rod to the push of the spring gales.

Just now, before the full masking of the new leaves, I find it amusing to see how my garden birds cheated me last spring, for in the shrubberies and bounding hedges I see nests which I never knew were there. I even missed the nest of a blackbird built in the rose creeper by my front door and I only came upon it last week when I went to prune the branches!

SPRING

The Promise of Spring

Yes! There is no doubt about it, the evenings are drawing out! What an obvious, trite, observation to make! Yet there is magic in those words. No longer do I have to draw the curtains at four o'clock in the afternoon or, if I happen to be working on a painting, to put my brushes away at half past three. Some painters work by artificial light, that I cannot do. My studio light faces north and at mid-winter painting hours are short.

Already I can sense a certain promise, as though the winter earth stirs and sighs in its sleep. This is only noticeable in the early twilight, let us say, half an hour before 'ducking' time (though the wild quackers are safe for another year).

A faint air of mystery steals about my garden and pool (so lately sheeted with thick ice). Under the old apple trees and the thick shrubberies behind, the dusk seems to gather like a mist. Blackbirds, all cocks, run about on the lawn, warily eyeing each other like rutting stags, for it is now time to stake out territories; I have yet to hear that faint low warble of the blackbirds in the twilight; I listen for it as I listen for the cuckoo, as yet such a long time away, nine weeks? Ten?

Not a breath of wind moves in the dark line of firs which mark the boundary of my property. The voices of children playing in the village street come faintly, that's another sign of the turn of the year.

With my binoculars I look across to the forest. Through the magic lenses I can clearly see the pigeon dropping down into the larches and the slow walk of pheasants as they gradually draw in to their roosts. What a wonderful invention this is, the binocular! You can play Peeping Tom on many a wild creature which you cannot even see with the naked eye. Two cock pheasants are sparring by the wood edge, jumping like farm-yard cocks and striking with their spurs. Moving the glasses a little to the left I can see the buff dead grass lining the distant hedgerow.

There is something sitting in the grass. It is a rabbit. It seems to be watching the sparring pheasants.

To the naked eye this rabbit was quite invisible. Where the oak trees hang over the winter wheat, which is now well up and green, there is something else moving, a grey squirrel. It bounds about with an arched back, then sits up suddenly, paws to mouth. But the evening is late, it does not linger. I see it dart up the oak trunk and vanish.

Look now to the forest across the wide meadow. It looms as a dark mass of shadow, each individual tree melting into the whole. A white mist steals over the winter wheat. I can hear the far-away calling of the owls, always vociferous at this time of year. Only a week ago, on just such a quiet gloaming, I heard the asthmatic bark of a fox. How safe the foxes are in these great woods! They at least give the Woodland Pytchley some exercise, for hounds are lucky if they ever manage to get a fox away; they spend their time running the rides, here, there, everywhere.

Over the apple tree, a star burns steadily; now the lingering twilight has deepened to night much of the magic seems to have gone.

Is it the promise of spring which holds me at this time? The thought of the returning sun, the dragonflies flitting over the moorhens' pool, of the westward-facing wall, where my peach tree grows, which is almost too hot to touch after a day of summer sun? No, it is not the looking forward, it is the satisfaction of sensing the first stirrings of the earth, happening at this instant, and very soon now I shall catch the scent of the growing grass.

The other day I visited the Welney Washes Wildfowl Trust. This proved to be an experience which I shall never forget, and if this sounds too extravagant a statement, let me describe what I saw.

Despite ominous weather forecasts the night before which gave dire warnings of heavy snow and drifting, and I know not what else, I set off with two friends and daughter Angela. As we entered those flat lands of the fens (which always fill me with wonder that anyone could live in such a treeless, woodless land), the sun came out and sparkled on the frosty wayside grass and ice-sheeted flood waters at Earith.

We reached the Trust at midday, and, as daughter Angela is a member we were able to enter the wonderful warm viewing room with its comfortable chairs and panoramic windows. The sunlit scene before us, as we parted the heavy curtains, and entered that room, was absolutely breathtaking. All the great expanse of the Washes was sheeted in ice. Below the windows there was open water and three small islands, slabsided with ice sheets. Each island was crammed to overflowing with water-fowl, chiefly pochard, mallard and coots. All around was a great company of wild swans, some asleep on one leg (the leg at an acute angle to give correct balance), others were eating potatoes on the ice, a difficult feat for as they leant forward, stretching out their long white necks, the potatoes skidded on before them. The big birds staggered all over the place with their huge black paddles slipping beneath them.

Some were asleep just below the windows; through my glasses I could bring them within a few feet of me. The icy wind rippled in their snowy feathers like a wind passing over a field of moving grass. And how their brilliant canary-yellow bills stood out against the black V pattern!

What a vast contented company this was, spread out before us! A truce declared on both sides between bird and bird, and man and bird, no danger here of guns or nets. I was struck at once by the sense of good fellowship and happiness in that great throng. There were no uneasy glances alert for danger, every bird knew it was safe and, incidentally, that from some mysterious source food would be provided. Each duck and swan was in immaculate plumage, not a feather out of place, many looked as though they were carved out of smooth marble or close-grained highly polished wood.

As far as the eye or binocular could range there were birds, all truly wild, mark you. Two lovely pintail were resting on a spit of land and beyond them a pack of wigeon. Not a moment passed but some fowl were in the air, swans beating heavily along, white against the blue winter sky, teams of wigeon hurtling to and fro. The sun made a brilliant green metallic dazzle on the mallard drake's heads and gave an almost autumn gold hue to the heads of the pochard.

What an absolute treat this scene was for anyone interested in birds, whether sportsman or naturalist.

Blackbirds and Butterflies

I heard the first spring warble of the blackbird on the morning of February 23, just before sunrise. I listen for this hint of spring as eagerly as I look for the first swallow. The savage frost had eased at last and my garden pool, where my moorhens breed each summer, which had been sheeted with bearing ice for many days, had begun to melt.

My resident moorhens, which had been with me since the autumn, and had stayed until the pond froze, showed up briefly as soon as the thaw came. They inspected the pond, walked about on it, and departed again. Now they are back, and before many days have passed they will be thinking of building their nest. Last year, being an open winter, they had eggs by the end of March but not so this year. For one thing the clump of reeds in which they build is not yet high enough to form a screen, but it is good to see them back. They spend the day swimming, preening on the banks, and now and again there is a 'chase me Charlie' round the apple trees.

Looking back at the recent severe snows (though we were free of it in the central Midlands), I cannot help wondering how many of the small birds perished, particularly the wrens and woodpeckers. The most killing time of all for the insect-eating birds is when frozen mist and rain cloaks the tree bark, enclosing the crevices with an armour plating of ice. The long-tailed tits also perish in prolonged cold weather, so do countless field-fares and redwings. I noticed many of the latter too weak to fly, stumbling desperately about in the frozen fields, so feeble that some tipped forward on their beaks.

A kindly fruiterer in our local market town gave me, free of charge, a big bag of white grapes. These proved a godsend to the blackbirds, thrushes and redwings. They gobbled down the grapes in frantic haste. Cut-up apples were equally popular, and of course I kept the tits supplied with nuts hanging from the bird table close to my window. At one time I counted over thirty tits, great tits and blue tits, and the odd greenfinch, all feeding at once. Now, in the gentler weather, the surviving birds are getting down to the business of mating and singing, and before March is out we should hear the first chiffchaff in the forest near my house.

Last month whilst the very hard weather was at its worst I had a visit from a snipe which hunted round the frozen margins of the pool without much success. It then stood disconsolately on the ice, very puffed up and wretched before it flew away.

It is amazing what a variety of birds I have had visiting this garden pool. The list includes heron, kingfisher (a frequent visitor who has cleared a smaller pond close by of minnows), snipe, wild mallard – a pair which arrived three mornings running just after the thaw, moorhen, and a single teal. Considering this pool is within ten feet of my house it shows how water attracts birds and in the heat of summer the larks come in from the fields to drink and bathe.

But to return to the subject of blackbirds. Though they will strip the strawberry bed and raspberry rows I delight to have them in my garden. Their warbling song is more agreeable to my ear than the singing of the nightingale, for it has a dreamy quality about it, evocative of summer heats and green shades of the forest. And when next you see a cock blackbird in full plumage, notice the quality of that black plumage. It has not the metallic sheen of the rook or magpie. It is one of the most beautiful blacks in nature; it is not absolutely black, there is a very dark brown tinge in it, it is not a blue black. What delight there is in that beautiful corn-gold bill of the cock; what better colour could contrast with that soft black plumage! It is a more splendid contrast than the red beak of the chough.

Blackbirds are most particular over their territory, like the robin. Early in the year, when the weather is mild, one can see them running about the gardens and parks, sometimes as many as a dozen or more. It is a sort of mating ritual, akin to the displaying of the blackcock or the ruff. Occasionally furious battle is joined and feathers fly. The cock blackbird is a pugnacious creature and will harry the gentle song thrushes which come for the apple slices.

Each year the blackbirds build in a porch creeper by my front door, sometimes having two broods in the same nest, especially if I remove the old soiled lining after the first brood has flown.

Watching the tits busy over the peanut bags I pondered on the subject of colouring in birds. Blue is an unusual colour in birds' plumage, only the jay shows it on his wing and, of course, the kingfisher and the blue tits. So many people never notice the little miracles of nature. Take the blue of the blue tit's crown, what a wonderful colour it is: the blue of an April sky! The Americans call the tit family chickadees and, like us, they have several species. How strange it is that whilst four of our resident species are hole-dwellers, two, the longtailed and bearded tit, build substantial nests in bushes or reed beds.

Every year, in the lane opposite my house I can rely on finding three or four nests of longtailed tits. This lane adjoins the forest; I have never found a nest in the woods, always in the blackthorns which hedge the lane. Foolishly, they build before the leaves are open and most are found by the jays who systematically hunt the hedges. The nests stretch like an elastic bag. They have need to, for the young are numerous and both parents roost with their chicks at night.

I am not a good enough ornithologist to tell a marsh tit from a willow tit, and I have never seen either a bearded tit or a crested tit though I have been to localities where they occur.

If you wish tits to breed in your garden it is no use putting up nest boxes in April. They must be in place soon after Christmas, for the old birds start house-hunting very early and by the end of this month most sites will have been thoroughly inspected and chosen. Usually the nest box should be placed facing north.

When the young are ready to fly they will choose a favourable morning, like bees do when they swarm. Then, strangely, once out of the nest, they seem to disperse far and wide and are not seen again. They are quite capable of looking after themselves and after a few hours appear to be quite independent of their parents.

In my garden I have a young sallow tree enclosed in a fine muslin cage to keep out spiders and earwigs and other vermin. The silver buds are now just beginning to show. During the arctic conditions the twigs and buds were glazed with ice and I wondered how my hibernating larvae of the purple emperor butterflies were faring. I need not have bothered. These tiny larvae, smaller than the silver buds, are beginning to turn a pale shade of green, matching their surroundings like chameleons.

One or two chose a dead and dried sallow leaf on which to hibernate, and what a wonder was there; despite tremendous buffeting by winter gales which stripped tiles off the houses in the village those leaves held firm to the parent stalk, secured by a gossamer binding of thread cunningly woven by the larvae in October days. I do not know as yet how many I have upon this little tree for it takes the eye of a titmouse to detect them. Some hibernate in a crinkle of the bark, some go low down on the main stem, their colour exactly matching the colour of the bark. As soon as the tender green leaves split from the silver buds they will awake and wander, but now, in these cold March days, they are still asleep.

Once the leaves have opened they will grow and shed their skins, growing larger every week, until by June they are great handsome larvae as long as my thumb, carrying upon their heads two stately horns like little bulls. By the end of June they will have pupated and in early July will emerge as glorious butterflies to be released in their sanctuary. How much better that they should fly free in the great oak woods (though they are seldom seen) than pinned upon a collector's setting board. On

48

rare occasions when the July sun beats down upon the ridings one can glimpse them soaring high up around the oak crowns, truly emperors of our ancient English oak forests.

The Creeping Tide

I take a keen delight in seeing the first signs of the coming spring. They are at first so subtle that your average country-dweller fails to notice them. One feature is the skirmishing of cock blackbirds on the garden lawn or in some sheltered meadow corner by the wood. In late February and March one sometimes sees as many as a dozen or so, all cocks hopping around each other and occasionally engaging in brief and bloodless combat.

Of the hens there is no sign. Maybe they are watching the sparring of their favourite Black Princes from the shadow of the nearby hedge, but in any case, hens of the bird world take little notice of the antics of the cocks. I have seen a party of varicoloured ruffs in Friesland going through the most absurd gyrations, while nearby the drab little hens were busy feeding (or were they, with true feminine cunning, taking appraising side-glances at the valiant knights?).

Robins, too, are active, staking breeding territory. When it is almost dark (I would describe it as flighting time for the goose and duck hunter), when the far shrubberies in my garden are seen as through a glass darkly, then I hear the very low and muted warblings of the cock blackbirds trying out a few staves, like an orchestra tuning up their instruments. To me, the song of the blackbird is the most evocative and lovely of all the songs of British birds. It is the last sound I would wish to hear when the hour arrives for my departure from this very beautiful world. It has the quality of a woodwind instrument.

A cock blackbird, when he is a really good vocalist (and all birds vary in their rendering of song just as humans do) is really something to listen to.

This brings me to another subject, and that is how difficult it is in this modern age to obtain real quiet and freedom from the sound of man's restless activity as he goes about his business. This fact was borne in upon me not so long since, when I was

endeavouring to record the song of our resident nightingale. It was almost impossible to find a moment when there was not some disturbing growling of traffic, motors on the distant road, tractors ploughing, aeroplanes buzzing – it was quite maddening.

Perhaps it was this experience which made me wish to move to some part of Britain where one can enjoy the silences, silences which are broken only by natural sounds of birds, the wind in the trees and grass, the talk of streams, or the respiration of the sea.

It is not generally realised what few places remain from, let us say, Inverness to Lands End, where one can get away from the noise of machines. It is only on the wilder moors and high hills where one can be rid of it.

We have come to tolerate noise, the louder the better, especially for the youth of today. The louder the motor cycle, the more raucous the disco music, the more it pleases.

It is the less obvious signs of coming spring that I look for: the first coltsfoot pretending to be a dandelion (which latter flower will not be seen until May), the first green shoots of the dogs mercury in the woodland and, later, the frail wood anemone.

My moorhens have become very active, the cock chasing his wife around the apple trees, fanning his snow-white tail, bending his head until the beak touches the ground, and turning that dazzling white fan towards her. They tickle each other's necks in a most gentle fashion, taking it in turns to present their black napes to one another. If and when I move to my dream mill house I shall be tempted to take them with me, but I have not yet got around to a method of catching them up. We are now such good friends I feel I might lose their trust. In a curious way these sooty rails have become part of the family.

Yet, who knows? Should I find my mill house and its accompanying mill pool I might persuade them to remain with us, even in a strange county. Or maybe the pull of their birthplace would be too strong and they would fly away.

I cannot help looking back to boyhood days when my brother and I used to hunt moorhens with bow and arrow. Their habit of diving and hiding when scared was all part of the hunt. We became as keen and knowledgeable as otter hounds in tracing the silver bubbles of an underwater victim. With long practice we could usually spot the scarlet bill hiding under flood rubbish or weed. Once despatched they were plucked and roasted, and very good they were too. The close black wool is most difficult to pluck. The best way to deal with it was to use a blow lamp. Gently roasted in a covered tin for about twenty minutes they were far better than snipe and an equal to woodcock.

Any day now I shall see the first honeybee round the yellow crocus. The first crocus to show in my garden was at the beginning of February; no doubt there were much earlier ones in the London parks. I have yet to catch that first faint perfume of growing grass and herbage waking from its winter sleep. One notices it first when the sun shines on a March morning, usually on some sunny bank or in the lee of a wood. Yet what a feeble thing is our modern spring compared with those of thirty years ago.

The chiffchaff comes to the woods but how seldom is he heard, the frogs and toads have gone, so have the whitethroats from the hedgerows, and the cuckoo, when he does arrive, is heard for only a week or so then falls victim to the farmers' toxic sprays. The wireworm was a favourite food for the cuckoo, and so were the numberless insects to be found in the growing grass and crops. It does not take very long to silence that voice which surely set a seal to the British spring.

All this may seem a melancholy summing up, yet I fear it is true; so much seems on the debit side, so little on the credit. Yet I will end on two bright notes. Last week I saw a large flock of cock chaffinches and larks, and the English partridge is making a good recovery.

Spring is Here

Come with me this March evening into Hammer Wood. The keeper told me that there were some pigeon in, quite an event for my part of the world. During the fierce February snows I saw a few flocks eating the kale, but even the kale was soon stricken by the savage frost, as was all my sprouting broccoli which I was nurturing for the spring. Those flocks of starved birds soon passed on elsewhere, possibly to west and south.

Hammer Wood is composed of oaks, fine big trees, and quite a lot of sallows where in the last century purple emperors were found, but not now. Spraying for *tortrix* some twenty years ago killed them; not one has been seen since. How I love the oak woods! With old John Clare, the eighteenth-century poet (who lived not so far away to the east of us) I could sing 'all day long I love the oaks'. Let us hope and pray that the oak disease which is now prevalent in the USA and is, from all accounts, as deadly as the elm disease, is kept out of this country. We should be as vigilant over this as we are about rabies.

The path I followed was printed with the neat cloven spoor of fallow deer and muntjac but, praises be, no horses had come this way, punching holes in the soft clay. Everywhere there was the promise of spring, I could smell it in the air, that subtle perfume which is so hard to describe. There were even yellow buds on the primrose clumps and the dogs mercury was transforming the woodland floor. Later there will be sheets of wild garlic and bluebells. Truly these days of very early spring lend a magic to the great oak woods of the Midlands.

I turned aside from my narrow path and, with Polar my labrador at my heel, sought some suitable hide within reach of the taller oaks and poplars. This was not easy. The underwood was sparse and gave scant cover – mostly hazels and blackthorn, no dense bushes. If you have a rifle it is necessary to be well concealed. (I was carrying my little German .22, a beautiful

54

weapon with a telescopic sight and some nicely grained wood for the stock.) With a shotgun this is not so essential, as your shots will be at pigeon as they fly over the tree tops.

I pushed about among the thorns and hazels until I spied the very place. Three ash poles grew close together and up these, helped by a leaning ragged blackthorn bush, a honeysuckle had climbed and formed a natural tent. Already up its twisting vines the small green leaves were bursting forth. Honeysuckle is an early sprouter and puts forth leaves long before other woodland shrubs. Here then was an ideal ambush. From it I could command at least five 'sitty' trees, all oaks, some with ivy on them, always a draw for pigeon, for they like to roost in an ivy-clad tree and they also devour the berries in winter which form good iron rations. This honeysuckle bower was in a delightfully remote part of this great wood. I found it hard to believe that only a few short weeks ago the snow lay drifted here and the wood itself was completely cut off by mountainous drifts.

I sat down on my shooting stick to wait results and mean-while could make a careful study of the scene before me. No sign yet of the oaks in bud. Usually at this time of the year at winter's end there is a reddish hue on the tree tops, but not now. It was one of those evenings when there is no definite light in any part of the sky. The clouds were high and withdrawn – only a shade more luminous towards the sun's setting. Little birds were active in the tops of the oaks, either tits or redpolls; I did not have my glasses with me.

Not far off a mistlethrush started to sing, bold fluting notes with a wild ringing quality, resembling the song of the black-bird in some of its phrases but much more vibrant, a song which carries for a considerable distance on a still evening. It was some time before I could locate the chorister. At last I spied the big bold thrush sitting on the very top of an ash tree some hundred yards away. He sang continuously for over twenty minutes, repeating the same phrase over and over again. Somehow that song matched the great winter-weary woodlands.

The first customer came unannounced and as a complete surprise. One moment the oak top was bare, when next I looked, there sat a woodie. Its head was craning about as it looked round, for no bird save crow or magpie, is so wary. I kept quite still even though I was sure it could not see me, and after a close scrutiny it settled down on its twig and puffed itself out, wobbling its crop. I gave it another minute or so to get settled then edged the little rifle to my shoulder. When I looked through the cross threads I found there was a slender wriggly branch of oak right across the target, a hopeless shot, so I waited for the pigeon to move. I had not been waiting more than a minute or so when another came sweeping down with set wings. It had seen the bird on the bough. It alighted on another topmost twig just above the first customer. One peep through my scope and I saw it was clear of any twig. The range was about eighty yards or so, not a difficult shot if I held the rifle steady. I got the cross thread on its chest and was about to squeeze the trigger when both birds started up with a great clatter and vanished.

I couldn't believe that they had seen me and wondered if the keeper was walking up the main ride. He knew I was coming and was no doubt following my tracks. All was quiet. The mistlethrush departed, and the only sound was the thin wailing of the lambs.

At this season of the year, when the evenings begin to lengthen, that period between five o'clock and seven seems to linger interminably, the sun seems to refuse to sink and there is little change in the colour of the sky. Looking at my watch I saw it was nearly six o'clock. If the big flocks were coming, it must surely be soon. Polar sat beside me like a dog carved out of stone, only occasionally turning his head, sometimes to look at me, and then lowering his gaze to look along the forest floor where the dead oak leaves still lay. All of a sudden there was a sibilant rushing sound. The sky above me was filled with birds.

The pigeon wheeled around with set wings, alighting clumsily with much clatter and clapping in the oak tops. Some were directly above me, others clustered like grey fruit on the oak-tree crowns. I gave them time to have their look around, then chose a bird which was outlined on top of an oak on my right. At the shot there was a frantic clatter of wings as the whole flock took off. The bird I had fired at remained quite immobile for a second then slowly heeled over and hit the dead oak leaves some seventy yards off.

Polar was away like a greyhound and came back with it, a surprisingly fat pigeon, for most have not yet recovered from the big snows. There followed a longish wait. Then two stock doves came and settled in the tree directly above me. I judged that they might act as decoys and so it proved, for some five minutes later six woodies came in and settled in range on the oak tops. My crumb of lead again sped true and a second bird dropped to the woodland floor.

I sensed that the best time was past, only an odd late pigeon was likely to come in. But I stayed on until the light went. Gradually a dimness settled over the great wood. Pheasants cocked to roost, the little lambs fell silent. Only two pigeons for a two-hour wait! No matter. There is something enjoyable in a big oak wood on a March evening. Far away an old tawny began to hoot, or it may have been a long-eared owl, for there is a pair or two in this wood. No doubt the deer would be leaving their harbours in the dense thickets, and the night people, badger and fox, would be sniffing the evening air.

It was almost dark by the time I reached the hunting gate and lifted the latch, and there in the lee of the wood was a bat patrolling up and down, the first I had seen since autumn. Truly spring is here!

Rooks and Frogs

The rooks are busy now. March is an important month for them and I have been watching them about their nests. Some have already been completed and a black wedge tail could be seen sticking over the rim with the male bird standing guard. There was an awful lot of thieving going on, birds waiting until the industrious owners of a half-built nest had departed for more material and then sneaking up and wrenching away a twig. If the rightful owners arrived during this thieving process violent quarrels took place and I saw two birds locked in combat, almost falling to the floor of the rookery, each swearing away as only the crow family can.

One or two ancestral nests which had survived all that the winter storms could throw at them had a new one built on the top. In time these twiggy structures, so cunningly woven in and out, become top-heavy and fall to the ground. I noticed that live twigs are sought after, the birds clumsily hopping on to the thinner twigs and twisting them off with their powerful bills.

I have a great regard for the rook and, though as a youngster I used to enjoy rook shooting with a .22, I hate to see them shot in these lean years for the population is at least half what it was twenty years ago. This is due to the pesticides which kill their favourite food. The damage they do is outweighed by the good, and the English countryside without the rook would be a still more barren place for the naturalist.

I watched some of the birds striding sedately about in the adjoining meadow, and through my binoculars I could see they were twisting off dead grass bents for nest lining. I once had a pet rook called Percy. I had found him as a fledgling fallen from the nest, a pathetic bundle huddled among the dog's mercury and I took him home and reared him. I learnt a lot about rooks. He was very attached to me, following me about wherever I went, and to show pleasure he erected his head feathers and bowed and swayed and even treated me to a funny little musical song. I had never realised before that rooks could sing (so can the jay, though one seldom hears a jay singing).

Percy slept in a box lined with hay which was kept in the stables. I never clipped his wings but he seemed unable to fly more than a few yards; his wing must have been damaged in his fall from the nest. Now the interesting thing about this bird was the way he knew when I was coming home from business. Every evening at around five o'clock he would be waiting for me in the drive, just as a dog waits for his master's home-coming.

When he saw me he would wag his wings and caw, bowing to the ground. I became absurdly attached to Percy. Then one day I saw no little black gnome awaiting me at the white gate and for a week I mourned for him. I searched high and low all about his favourite haunts, one of which was the lamp room. In those days we had no electric light and the large house was lit by oil lamps and candles. Percy had his favourite perch beside the oil drum on the bench, where, each morning, the domestics cleaned and filled the numerous paraffin lamps, a messy and smelly job.

And then one evening, when I was walking round the shrubberies still hopefully calling his name, I heard a feeble croaking 'caw'. There was my old pal with a dreadfully mangled wing. Some wretched cat or dog had set on him. No doubt he had fought off his enemy with has powerful bill but not before he had been dreadfully mangled. I took him up and nursed him back to health, but thereafter he would not venture outside the yard door or down the gravel drive. Then, unknown to me, the gardener put down some rat poison. Percy ate some. I found him dead in his box. The shock of his death was very real to me. One gets so attached to wild creatures which one has reared.

In the old days no gentleman's residence was complete without a rookery in the grounds. In some books published in the eighteenth and early nineteenth century there are suggestions as to how a landowner could induce the birds to nest in his park. Most of the suggestions are absurd, such as tying 'bundles of sticks' to the tree tops, or tying young rooks to makeshift nests placed up in the trees.

There seems to be no shortage of rooks in Scotland. Last autumn I saw vast flocks wheeling about their roosting woods just as I used to see them in the Midlands of England. When the old birds are feeding their young it is amusing to see them flying to the tree tops with their grey skin pouches weighed down with grubs reminding one of small black pelicans.

One of the most familiar sounds in March used to be the croaking of the mating frogs in every field pond. How I miss those drums of spring! Two years ago I heard one croaking in my big pond. He kept it up night and day for a week or more, but no other frog appeared, and after a heron visited us early one morning, I heard no more resonant croaking. It is a sound which carries a considerable distance and I imagine frogs can hear each other, though how much a frog can hear has never been ascertained.

The mating season coincides with the hatching of the young herons. I used to find the frog skins neatly scraped clean lying around the margins of the ponds. It is many years since I saw those countless numbers of baby frogs making for the water; one always had to look where one put one's feet. This migration always took place after heavy rain, which gave rise to the country belief that they fell from the clouds.

There are still some pockets in the Midland countryside where one can hear the chorus of the March frogs, but they are few and very far between, usually in the suburbs of towns where the agricultural sprays have not done their deadly work.

Pike will take a frog as readily as they will a roach. When we were boys we had an old gardener called Perkins who was a great sportsman. My brother and I thought he was a wonderful man. He used to take us pike fishing every Saturday afternoon to a large square pool in the park. We caught live bait from a fallen willow at one end, but roach were not always easy to come by and then Perkins looked about for a dead frog which was threaded on his big treble hooks. This often proved a deadly bait. Foxes will hunt round the margins of ponds when the frogs are mating in spring and eat them.

Last summer I noticed my moorhen family all gathered in a circle on my lawn: Pa, Ma and their six children which had been hatched on the pond at the end of May. They were looking at something and now and again they would spring back. I was intrigued by this and went out to investigate. The moorhens ran off and there was a frog. Each time it had jumped the moorhens had jumped back in alarm.

I picked it up and carried it to the pond. I doubt very much whether a moorhen would eat a frog but it is possible. One hapless fledgling blackbird which could not fly was attacked by my adult moorhens and killed. They are pugnacious birds and once, when a strange moorhen came into the garden, there was a spectacular fight under the apple trees, both birds turning on their backs and striking each other with their claws. I have seen them attack young ducklings and drown them. No other bird, blackbird, thrush, or other moorhen, is allowed near my pond when the pair is in residence, they guard their territory with great ferocity.

Vanishing Butterflies

In the April sunshine, on the southern edge of Bullocks Wood, I watched that first butterfly of spring, a yellow brimstone. In actual fact I saw my first brimstone in March during that delightful spell of weather which brought out the golden crocus in all the parks and gardens. I greatly admire the brimstone, not only for that clear primrose colour of the wings, which matches so well the primrose clumps in the woods, but also for the lyre-shaped wings which no other British butterfly can match.

My particular brimstone by Bullocks Wood was revelling in the gentle warming rays, flitting in and out between the hazel stems where the green dog's mercury was already hiding the bare woodland floor. Eventually it came to rest on a dead stalk of grass and spread its wings, luxuriously as a cat stretches before a fire.

Some years ago I watched the mating flight of two brimstones in my garden on a warm March morning. The female ascended high into the sky with the male in attendance, just as the female purple emperor soars skywards when mating. Then down she came in a steep dive and hid herself in an ivy-clad archway. The male followed, and there they mated. The interesting fact is that they remained in coition for four days. This surely must be unusual in a butterfly, though there is one recorded instance of a pair of brimstones being in coition for a fortnight.

Altogether, it's a curious insect. It goes into hibernation soon after emergence from the chrysalis in late summer, July and August, and therefore it has a long sleep until the following March. This accounts for the perfect condition of many of the spring brimstones. They invariably choose ivy for hibernation and their resemblance to the underside of the ivy leaf is one of the miracles of camouflage. The food plant is the alder buckthorn, though the brimstone will also select the purging buckthorn, that hedgerow bush which has large glossy black berries but

which the birds will not touch. Neither bush is common, and for that reason one may see the brimstone travelling many miles in spring, plodding along the sides of the hedges and lanes. The caterpillar is a soft velvety green which matches exactly the colour of the buckthorn leaf.

Like the brimstone, the small tortoiseshell is another butterfly of early spring and, like the brimstone, it hibernates, often coming into houses in late summer where it likes to rest on curtains. But many of these spring tortoiseshells are not in the immaculate condition of the brimstones. The very rare large tortoiseshell, which is so seldom seen now, and which is probably counted as one of our rarest British butterflies, is a lovely insect with all the rich browns and reds of an Indian carpet. I have only seen one once in my life and that was down a drove in Wicken fen where there was an avenue of elms. The larvae feed on elm, always at the top of the tree, though sometimes they have been found on sallows and willows.

I remember that fine Norfolk naturalist Ted Ellis telling me he once found a mass of large tortoiseshell larvae on a willow when he was voyaging down a Norfolk creek. Not being a collector he left them there, but I would have been sorely tempted to take them to 'bring them through' for release, as the larvae are the special prey of ichneumon flies. A friend told me last year that he saw a large tortoiseshell in a west-country walled garden where it was feeding on Michaelmas daisies. He was so excited he rushed home some miles distant for his camera and when he returned the butterfly was still there and he took a photo of it.

At one time the tortoiseshell was not at all uncommon around London and the Midlands but it began to disappear about thirty years ago. Why this should be is a mystery, and the same applies to the lovely silver-washed fritillary which is one of our most beautiful butterflies. I have seen the brambles on the rides of Salcey Forest in Northamptonshire absolutely glowing with these golden-winged creatures, but one rarely sees them now.

The same may be said for many of our once-common butter-flies. Many can remember the waysides of country lanes alive in summertime with the bobbing flight of uncountable thousands of meadow browns. They have gone, along with the lovely little blues and small coppers.

Now that was a little gem which fascinated me as a boy! That small jewelled insect whose outside wings were as attractive as the inside, but which was outshone by the very rare large copper which now only survives in the fens under rigid protection and careful conservation. It was there one lovely summer day that I saw what I thought was a glowing coal in the middle of a bush; when I came close I saw it was a large copper sunning itself. When it flew it was transformed into a blue butterfly for the underside wings are a metallic blue, more noticeable in flight than when at rest. I talked with the warden of the reserve and he told me what a struggle they have to keep this species going as it feeds on the water dock and this is frequently submerged by floods, and although the larva can apparently stay submerged for a considerable time, prolonged floods will kill it.

The gradual disappearance of our native butterflies, as well as some birds and plants, is one of the most worrying things today. Even the red admiral, once so plentiful in our gardens in later summer, seems to be becoming scarce. I saw only four or five last year. Can the cause be that our climate is changing, or that we are polluting the atmosphere and the land? The disappear-ance of the meadow browns can be explained by the spraying and cutting of roadside verges, and the spraying of crops and woodland trees.

Some thirty years ago I saw as many as ten or a dozen purple emperors on the wing in Salcey Forest but this insect seems to have disappeared entirely from the forest since the oaks were sprayed for tortrix. Yet a friend of mine who went to the south of France last summer told me that it was just like old times.

There were butterflies everywhere, and the waysides and

woodlands were alive with all the old familiar species.

A certain south country forest I know, where the purple emperor still occurs, is now under threat. When I last journeyed there I found that the sallows bordering the rides were being cut down. I am doing what I can to remedy the situation.

Along with the butterflies, the crickets and grasshoppers have vanished. A walk in a meadow thirty years ago meant grasshoppers jumping in front of you at every step. You do not see them now. All the richness and beauty which I remember is being eroded. This is very sad.

Of course I realise there are many people who could not care one jot if the purple emperor went, together with all the frogs, insects, plants and animals threatened by modern inventions and discoveries. One thing I do know is that the countryside is an infinitely poorer place than it was when I was a boy, and though there is much on the credit side of the balance sheet, such as the advance in medicine and technology, I am fearful for the country-lover and his enjoyment of the natural world. If we could rid ourselves of this dreadful feeling of impotence when we see the destruction caused by modern methods of farming I should have more cause for hope.

But let me not end on such a pessimistic note. Any day now I should hear the cuckoo and see the first swallow, though these do not show up in any numbers in the Midlands until near April's end. The dour days of winter are behind us.

A Charming Case

Two years ago I found a plant of oxslip growing in a shady part of the forest. It had been partly scratched out of the ground by some animal, probably a badger hunting for worms, so I brought it home and planted it beside my small rockery pool between two rocks. It is sheltered by the house from the north and east winds and faces west.

I brought this plant home because it is by no means a common flower in the heavy clay of the Midlands, as it prefers chalky soils. But this little plant thrived between its two rocks, actually began to flower before Christmas and has been flowering ever since, even surviving the hard weather we had in February! This spring it is throwing up even more flower heads and, by my reckoning, it has had a flowering period of six months which is surely very unusual. I hope indeed it is a true oxslip, as I read that there is a false oxslip which is a cross between a primrose and a cowslip, and both flowers are common in that vicinity. I believe it takes an expert to tell the difference and I have small knowledge of wild flowers; I am more familiar with waterside plants and flowers.

Years ago I got some roots of bogbean growing in a mountain loch and these still grow in my large pool, though the moorhens pull them about dreadfully, as they have my water-lilies. One water-lily, a pygmy variety, I plucked – in dire peril – from a Sutherland loch. This throve in my pond and, before the advent of the moorhens was a mass of flowers in season. But I fear there is little left of it. One cannot have moorhens and water-lilies in a small pool and I would rather have my moorhens; the lilies only flower for a short time in the summer, and the moorhens are with me all the year. These pygmy water-lilies which grow in Highland lochs are most attractive. I once talked with a man who had a strange story to tell. I told him how I had got my Highland lily and he said that once, when walking the hightops,

67

he came on a loch in which grew small blue water-lilies. There is no blue water-lily on the British list, so I think he must have been confusing the flower with something else, though I know of no blue water plant save the water forget-me-not.

I once found a very beautiful and rare blue gentian on a Suffolk brick, and though I returned to the locality the following year, I could not find the exact spot. I came upon it when studying the stone curlew, a bird I had never seen and which I was lucky to find. I listened to its strange wild cry as it flew about in the dusk; this fluting call has the same elfin quality about it as that of the woodlark.

Two years ago a dead stone curlew was picked up in a field near Oundle. Luckily I heard about it and managed to obtain it from the man who had found it in a furrow. I had it mounted by a local taxidermist to whom I gave a sketch of the pose, and a doctor friend made a case for it. I painted for a background a Suffolk brick, and placed the bird's feet among pebbles. It makes a charming case. I never realized that the stone curlew has no hind toe to speak of. Its plumage is a delightful harmony of browns, buff streaks and ivory shades, which exactly match the stony barrens of the brecks.

A really good taxidermist is hard to find, for a detailed knowledge of natural history is essential. How often one sees stuffed grebes and divers in impossible positions, standing up like partridges when, in real life, they can only shuffle along on their bellies and make a big business over that. I suppose the best taxidermists were Spicers, who once had a branch in Leamington. They did several things for me with the most artistic surroundings of dried grass and moss. A woodcock they did for me was mounted, crouched in oak leaves, with snow on the ground, the rich tones of the plumage matching the dead tones of the fallen leaves.

When I was a boy I found a dead wryneck lying in a Berkshire garden. I packed it up and sent it off to my old friend Geo Bazely who lived in Gold Street, Northampton. He was, I think, as good as Spicers for mounting birds, for he was a keen naturalist and sportsman. He made a splendid job of my wryneck despite the fact, he told me, that it was badly decomposed when it reached him. He also stuffed a Lilford owl for me, when I was a boy, which I shot with a .22 (scattering shot cartridge). This I still have.

Strange to say, I saw one of these pygmy owls in my garden only a week ago. I had not seen one for some years and it had evidently survived the hard February frosts. It is a good thing that all owls are protected these days, and also what a blessing it is that birds are no longer shot for 'casing'. My friend who stuffed my stone curlew showed me a magnificent tawny owl that he had mounted, which had been picked up dead in the road. The birds of prey, like some of the ducks, are not easy to skin for the skull will not pass through the neck.

I used to try my hand at taxidermy myself years ago and became skilful at skinning with a single incision under the wing. But I could not make a satisfactory body which is much more difficult. One very seldom sees a really first-rate example of the taxidermist's art; they nearly always fall down when it comes to setting the eyes in the head, invariably making them bulge out without setting them under the brow. This is especially noticeable in the birds of prey which have forbidding brows, and the actual eye should be turned slightly inwards towards the bill.

I managed to catch a magnificent sea trout in Loch Arkaig some years ago. I hooked it in the early morning far out on the loch (I was fishing from my boat) and when I felt for the net I found I had left it behind. So I had to drown the fish and beach it. I took it into Fort William and it was sent down to London by train that same day. This fish was beautifully mounted and I have it on my wall as I write this. It was nearly six pounds but there are very much bigger fish in Arkaig, including massive ferox. The keeper showed me a photo of one which was truly enormous; it weighed, if I remember rightly, close on seventeen pounds. Even a pike in prime condition can be a thing of beauty, and a friend of mine had one mounted which weighed close on twenty pounds. It was in the prime of condition with the primrose spots and bars on the flanks to prove it.

I have been keeping a sharp lookout for crossbills in the forest since I saw the two beautiful males before Christmas. I have a shrewd suspicion they nest in the conifers at the far end of the woods, but they prefer Scotch firs for nesting and this is a favoured tree in the Suffolk brecklands. It is a very early breeder, and they sometimes have young in the nest as early as February. It is something of a puzzle why crossbills choose to be so early, and the same applies to the raven and heron.

There is a heronry not far from my house, and at the beginning of March I saw the old birds standing around by their nests and by the end of the month they were sitting on eggs. All the fields around the heronry are being worked for gravel, and grabbers and cranes are working all day close to the heronry but I do not think the old birds are very disturbed, though perhaps fewer nests are occupied this year. The heron is an early breeder because the young are a long time in the nest so it is necessary to make an early start, but this does not apply to the crossbill and raven.

Though there has been such a drastic reduction amongst the birds of prey, the warblers and even the finch tribe (one never sees the large companies of chaffinch cocks in winter which I remember as a boy), the heron has been unaffected, at least in our part of the country, and in Norfolk it is as common as ever. As far as I can see the only birds unaffected by modern farming methods are the sparrow and the pheasant. There was a period during the unrestricted use of DDT when pheasants were found dead, but not in any great numbers. I well remember the first year the deadly sprays and dressings were used indiscriminately, for the woods were littered with thousands of dead birds: woodpigeons, finches, blackbirds and rooks. The rooks have never really recovered and the only large flocks of rooks I have seen have been in Scotland. Only last year I saw a newly sown field not far from my house littered with the bodies of rooks, poisoned by the dressing put on the seed. So the damage still goes on.

Golden Chieftains

Some miles to the east of my house is a high tract of country called the Wolds and even up to the last century the large blue butterfly was found there, together with the purple emperor in the adjoining oak woods. Both have now gone. The large blue was a fine race, larger than those found today in Gloucestershire and the coastal cliffs of Devon and Cornwall.

I remember the Wolds when they were uncultivated acres of rough grass and ant hills, and though I never saw the large blue there, it was a grand place for fritillaries, the high brown, dark green, and silver-washed. Then, in between the wars, this area came under the plough. Where once the lovely insects flew corn grows and sheep graze.

In the late spring I was passing through this area by car and was brought up short by the sight of innumerable dumpy birds scattered over a large field of springing oil rape. I always carry my binoculars with me and, stopping the car, I was able to feast my eyes on a really wonderful spectacle, a real bird watchers' bonus. For all these birds (and there must have been well over 500 on that field) were golden plover with the males in full breeding kit. Is there any more attractive member of the plover tribe? I doubt it, unless it be the grey plover. The males were dressed in velvety black gorget and upper breast with white or primrose facings; through the glasses their backs appeared as though truly fashioned in gold mail.

The strange thing about all the plovers is the way they feed. They seem to spend their time continually tripping along on twinkling legs and then stopping to look about them, remaining like little statues. Very rarely do they seem to put beak to ground, and when they do, having such short necks, they tip the whole body forwards as though bowing. The green plover has the same habit. What, I wondered, were they finding in this field of rape, was it grubs or insects? They will eat grasses and seeds but their main diet, according to Witherby's handbook, is insectivorous.

These golden plovers were extremely alert and wary. Now and again, if a car passed along the road, they were up in a body, wheeling with great precision, careering about the sky and then coming down again to rest, their pointed wings flickering and winnowing as they glided in.

A strange thought came to me as I watched this golden company. They were all so united; like a wandering Bedouin tribe they seemed to be a people of the wide open spaces. They were only encamped here for a brief time before they journeyed on, perhaps to the high moors of Yorkshire and the far Northlands. Many of our summer golden plovers arrive in this country in February and March before the big flocks break up and seek out their breeding areas. In winter it is rather a drab little bird without that wonderful velvet waistcoat, and as to grey plovers, I have only once seen one in breeding kit in Norfolk, and they do not go around in large flocks.

I do not know why the tribe I saw upon the high Wold made such a strange impression on me, somehow I felt they were much more intelligent and individualistic than our lapwings. Perhaps it was the way one or two of the male birds, standing like soldiers on parade, watching me in my car, were like little proud chieftains. The contrasting markings on the throat and breast made me think of a striking cobra with its hood spread.

In a few hours' time maybe the whole company would lift off and continue their way northwards to the wild high tops and rolling moors. Why is it that this plover is so shy of man? Is it because they are (I must confess it) excellent on the table? I am not sure I would shoot them now.

The green plover, due to protection, is now very common in the Midlands. Last winter I saw vast flocks over the ploughlands. When the chicks hatch anywhere near a road they tend to wander on to the hard surface and the parents have a terribly anxious time trying to take them to safety. Only last summer I saw a single green plover chick at the side of the main road near my house, with the mother bird braving the traffic by standing right in the centre of the white line, calling frantically. I went out of my house and took up the little chick and carried it to the centre of a ploughed field, with the mother diving and wailing above me.

Carrion crows and rooks are the greatest enemy of the nesting green plovers. They quarter the breeding grounds with great persistence, all the while being harried by the adult birds which dive down upon the black robbers, making them twist and swerve.

The magpie and jay show more sense, they sit in the boundary hedges and watch where the hen goes to sit in the scrape. It is not difficult to find the nest if you have a pair of good binoculars and a friend with you who will walk away from the breeding field while you remain in hiding. Before long the hen will run back to the nest scrape, though she may make several dummy runs to other scrapes to throw the watcher off the scent. But as soon as you see her settle down and remain in one spot, you can mark it with the eye in relation to the opposite boundary, a tree or bush, or clod of earth, and then walk straight to it.

Unfortunately, thousands of plovers' nests are wrecked each year by the modern methods of farming. When the field has been ploughed the roller will follow and, if wet weather intervenes and the roller is delayed, the eggs, laid in the plough, are then flattened later. Those nests in pasture stand a better chance, except for wandering stock. The chicks are wonderfully camouflaged and are exquisite little creatures. Many times when walking over the Wolds pursued by diving and screaming old birds I have almost put my foot on one of the babies tucked up in the grass absolutely motionless. When poked with the finger they get up and run with great swiftness even when just out of the egg.

The green plover has none of that fear of man displayed by its golden cousin and will sit in the plough within a few feet of you without moving. They are delightful birds, as are all the plover tribe, with their large gazelle-like eyes and slender dainty legs. The elegant crest of the green plover is a brilliant inspiration of Nature (or the Great Designer who, I like to think, arranges these things in the first place). The rufous red of the undertail covers, contrasting with the black and white tail, just sets off the whole ensemble. But I give the palm to their trim little golden cousins, the little proud chieftains of the high wild places.

Spring Thoughts

One of the most absorbing programmes on TV was that magnificent series *Life on Earth*, with David Attenborough. Anyone with any imagination at all could not help being fascinated by the mind-boggling history of life on this planet, from its very early beginnings to the present time. I was left with a strange sense of being privileged, even for a minute fraction of time, to be part of this stupendous, mysterious story. I had a sense of being one with every living creature, though it must be confessed I was glad that my ancestral beginnings did not lead me up the path of the hapless wildebeest or zebra, whose ultimate fate is to be pursued and throttled by lions and other meat-eaters. Yet the end usually came swiftly; it was all over within the space of minutes, a less lingering death than that which would be the lion's fate. I know that for me it opened my eyes even to the wonders of existence and the fearful majesty of nature. Even the sight of cheetah or lion racing flat out was a thing of beauty, those rippling muscles, the sense of vibrant power.

Some time ago, I was sitting by my pool one summer afternoon looking at a pussmoth caterpillar which was feeding on willow leaves. I had been watching over it for a number of days and seen it grow from a tiny wisp of larva to a well-grown handsome creature with its strange cat face and two rear tails. As I watched, I witnessed a dramatic incident which could be paralleled by the lion chasing and killing its prey. A wasp flew by. It had passed the willow leaf when it suddenly turned about and in an instance had pounced on the pussmoth larva and bitten off its head, flying away with the still writhing green body in its jaws. The attack was so sudden, like a flash of light, the whole incident could have been measured in fractions of a second. What, you may well ask, has all this to do with the country scene? More than you think perhaps. But let me get to the matter in hand.

An American friend, a Mr McMillan, sent me two inter-

esting features the other day; one concerned carp fishing, the other goose hunting in Nebraska, both articles illustrated by fine colour photos.

Like us, the coarse fishermen of America are becoming keen on carp because of the great size these fish can attain. In Mississippi a carp weighing 74 lb was caught by a man called Curtis Wade from Rankin County Lake. This was in 1963 and another, weighing over 55 lb, was caught in Minnesota in 1952. These were not mirror carp but full-scaled common, or, as I like to call them, 'monastic' carp. A fish I saw basking in Redmire was certainly in the region of 60 plus. When seen under the water, and close to the bank, fish appear much smaller due to distortion (and by that I do not mean to imply any lack of truth in the beholder). Carp of 90 lb have been reported by American net fishermen but I do not think our home-bred fish will ever attain that size. One thing is certain, if carp become too plentiful in a pond (and they breed very quickly in suitable warm waters) the size diminishes.

I seem to have earned – quite undeservedly – the title of the Father of Carp Fishers, because it was through me that Dick Walker first became interested, after reading my *Fisherman's Bedside Book* in which I dwelt at length on carp catching, and with Walker and some others we founded the Carp Catchers' Club. Now fishing for large carp is big business with a certain section of the angling fraternity, and there is that excellent magazine *The Carp* which appears from time to time with Peter Mohan as editor. It is some years now since I fished for carp; I was never anywhere near the First Division in the Carp Catchers' League as my best fish was only 15 lb. That weight would have been recorded with triumph some fifty years ago but not now; fish over 30 lb are caught by fishermen every year, and Dick Walker's own record of 44 lb has come close to being broken.

The mirror and scaleless carp, German bred, I believe, are hideous creatures resembling smooth, bloated, pickle barrels, but the common carp, from a clean water, is a ruggedly handsome fish mailed in glinting bronze scales, reminding one of the armour of a Norman knight.

As to goose hunting in the USA, this differs greatly from our own goose hunts. In the first place, the geese are usually Canadas, and the hunter spreads out a mass of decoys. In the picture I was sent there are at least forty visible. The bag is limited, as is the season.

Any day now I hope to see my first swallow. This will be a signal to take out the pane of glass in my garage door to allow them to go to and fro to their nests in the high rafters. And as I do so I think of the other end of the year, the solemn autumn day when that pane is put back and nailed in place, as sure a sign that summer is over as the putting back of the clocks to winter time.

Coax! Coax!

The other night I was reading myself to sleep, as is my habit. The village clock struck midnight. This told me two things: one, that the wind had gone round to the southwest, and two, that it was high time I finished my book and tucked my head into my wing. I was reading Col. Hawker's account of his great battle with Parson Bond, when he and some brother officers raided the unhappy clergyman's woods in pursuit of pheasants (Hawker was a brazen poacher).

I had just reached the part where the enraged cleric had 'eased himself with a vomit' when I heard something in the pool below my bedroom window which made me shut the book. It was the deep, oft-repeated 'coax! coax!' of a mating frog.

Now I have not heard that sound for two years, not since one solitary character haunted the Big Pond for ten days in the spring. It may come as a surprise to many readers why I was so astonished to hear that well-loved, well-remembered voice, for I understand there are still a few pockets in the country where frogs may be found. But around my house it is a very rare creature indeed, so different to, say, fifteen years ago when every field pond was alive with them in spring.

I turned out the light and lay listening to that calling voice (which carries a considerable distance) 'coax! coax! coax!' A solitary lovelorn frog calling for a mate. The bedroom window was open, the curtains drawn so that I could see the pale night sky and a trembling star. I could smell the cool night air also, so fragrant with the breath of late spring, and with that faint aroma of pond water, not stagnant muddy water, for I had now cleaned out the pond.

Listening to that rasping but not unmusical voice brought back memories of my old home where, each spring, the frogs came to the fish ponds below the park and how, one winter day, when the water was clear, I looked down and saw a rosette of sleeping frogs all arranged around the old decayed root of a water-lily, for they hibernate like this, breathing through their skins.

I remembered also how one of my fat carp fell victim to an amorous frog which had climbed on its back in the mistaken belief it was a lady frog. The hapless fish was in great distress for the frog had gripped it by the eye sockets and had forced its front 'knuckles' into the fish's eye. When I took fish and frog from the pond I had the utmost difficulty in making it release its grip.

There are many who shed no tears over the departure of the frog and toad, yet both creatures were the gardener's friend. My newly arrived visitor kept up its persistent chorus for a number of days and I did wonder if it was the same one which had visited my bog garden two years ago. The year before that, I had procured some spawn from a friend and had put this in a minor pool in my water garden where there were no fish.

The little pool soon became alive with tadpoles, but my moorhens were also in residence and they helped themselves; also the ferocious larvae of the water boatmen beetles and dragon fly killed a lot of them, for these creatures are deadly enemies of tadpoles and small fry, eating them alive. Moreover it is almost impossible to keep these pests out of a pond.

At my old home we had a pet toad who used to come nightly in high summer and somehow climb the flight of stone steps which led up to the front door, quite a feat of mountaineering. If there was a thunderstorm he was always waiting to be let in, where he hopped about the stone-flagged hall to the horror and consternation of the female members of the household staff. Frogs and toads, being cold-blooded creatures, live for many years, and I do not think their span of life has ever been calculated with any accuracy.

Springtime always brought a bonanza to the herons, who waited upon the amorous goings on in every wayside pool. They must have found the frogs a useful addition to their diet and a help with the feeding of their young, for the times coincided. The ability of frogs to remain under water is also found in snakes.

A grass snake which I once disturbed in the act of eating a frog retired in high dudgeon to the bottom of my ornamental pond and lay coiled on the mud for over a day. I get grass snakes in my present garden in hot summer weather and they enjoy swimming, taking a real delight in weaving their way from one side to the other. At my old home, there was a fine lake which I stocked with carp and trout, and I saw them every year on a hot day, swimming far out in the middle.

They move with considerable grace and speed, weaving their bodies in a steady whip-thong motion, their small nut-shaped heads being kept well above the surface. At such times they may well be taken by herons, though I have never come across an instance of this. The grass snake when cornered can emit a most repulsive and skunk-like smell which, if you get it on your clothes, is very difficult to erase.

No doubt the herons would not like this habit. How they ever manage to digest eels is a mystery, for the hapless victim is continually writhing, even when in the gullet and stomach of its captor, I have seen a heron battling with a very large eel on a Devon estuary and every time the bird managed to swallow the eel it kept on re-appearing through the bill.

Many fishermen make a great business over killing an eel. Nothing can better the method showed to me by, I think, Richard Walker, that is, to cut the eel behind the head with a very sharp knife so as to sever the vertebrae. It immediately goes limp with very little spasmodic writhing of the tail.

A lively eel on the end of your line, and its subsequent landing in the net, is a fearsome spectacle. The slimy convulsive writhing can entangle the line and net in a hopeless mess which takes hours to clean and unpick. Yet when you have caught your eel and suspended it by its neck from a stout hook you can put two pairs of pliers on the edges of the cut, and then with a gentle pull the slimy tough skin (which gives no purchase to the human fingers) rustles downwards like a glove finger, leaving the dry bluish boneless flesh which is so delicious to eat.

Many scorn to eat freshwater eels but they are quite marvellous. I prefer them to salmon if they come from a clean water. They are far superior in flavour to the conger and command high prices on fishmongers' slabs.

A Tragedy

I have a sad story to tell; I have suffered a great loss, a real tragedy, though other people may think it is of no consequence. From time to time I have described my family of moorhens which inhabit my garden pond, but to refresh your memory I had better begin at the beginning.

Three winters ago there appeared on my pool, a single hen moorhen. She came through the boundary hedge with all the wary caution of her breed and, seeing the coast was clear, swam about twenty yards from my french windows with one eye on the house.

I did not disturb her and kept out of sight. After a week or so she was a daily visitor. I put down chick crumbs, and eventually she came and fed. With the arrival of spring she appeared one day with a shy cock bird who soon settled down and came to be fed with her. Shortly after with the advent of the spring days, they began their courting and showed signs of nest building. They chose a clump of rushes growing in the pond and by the end of April the nest had been finished, the eggs had been laid, and the hen began to sit. With each day the pair became more friendly and came regularly to be fed. Before long the eggs hatched and the pond was dotted with the little black powderpuffs following the white flirting tails of their parents.

The brood grew rapidly, possibly helped by the daily handouts, for before many days had passed the parents brought along all seven chicks and a delightful thing it was to see the happy family so close to my windows. These soon were helping with the second brood, assisting to feed their new brothers and sisters. Moorhens do not place food direct into the bills of their offspring. Like the grebes they pick up a morsel and hold it out and the chicks take it. Both parents are marvellously gentle. If the chick fails to seize the tit-bit the first time the parent still holds out its bill without moving, giving the chick a second chance.

A Tragedy

By autumn, thirteen young had grown and were in full plumage. I could watch their attempts to fly, jumping up from the ground and ascending briefly like little helicopters. They also practised diving and swimming under water. But with the first frosts all were banished save one single chick, which they kept with them until the following spring. This too was sent packing as the days lengthened and nest building began again, in the same reed clump. After this brood hatched the hen built a second nest in the dense periwinkle plants by the second pond exactly opposite my windows, not ten feet away.

The young hatched. One night I heard a great disturbance; some rat or stoat, or possibly a cat, must have attacked them as they slept. But next morning all the young were still about so they had obviously saved themselves by diving. But that day both parents worked like beavers making another nest on the big pond, and that night took all the young to the new site, which was out in the water and safe from cats.

It was a delight to watch the fortunes of my happy pair who were absolutely devoted to one another. They would sit side by side tickling each other's neck and roosted side by side on the edge of the pond, two round balls of feathers in the beam of my torch when I went out to see all was well in the winter nights.

Last summer they reared fifteen young in three broods. Then came the spell of hard weather this winter when all the south country was buried in snow. We had no snow in the central Midlands but severe frosts. Both parents departed because the pond was locked in ice so thick that I could walk across it.

When the thaw came the moorhens returned. As spring ripened to summer they began to build their nest, once again in the rush clump. Father moorhen, always the most friendly, would come daintily down the lawn when I called him, his white tail fanned, so tame and glad to see me.

Then tragedy struck. A day or so ago I was mowing the lawn with my rotor mower. Just as I was finishing I saw the little hen slipping along behind the fir tree boundary but there was no sign of the male. Later that afternoon a passing friend told me he had just picked up a very big moorhen on the grass verge by my house. It had been struck by a passing motor and was dead, though still warm. It was my dear old pal. Now the little hen is desolate. She still hangs about the pond. The nest is deserted; there will be no little black balls of fluff to rejoice my eye. My daughter wept wild tears, I was near to it.

The insane rush of traffic these days will not pause if any bird is in the road. I always slow down, but not your average motorists – what does a bird or animal matter? I would never have believed I could have become so attached to wild birds as I was to my moorhen pair, though to many this will seem mere sentimentality, but there are some who will understand. I suppose that moorhens, blackbirds, yellow hammers, and hedgehogs are the most frequent victims on the roads of today, and to this we may add young rabbits. There is some evidence that hedgehogs are getting a little more traffic conscious and have learnt to run instead of to roll in a ball.

Blackbirds are most frequently run over in spring when they are engaged in warring with other cocks, pheasants are rather prone as well – in fact all the hen-footed birds are slow to learn, though one rarely sees a partridge casualty. Cats as a rule can look after themselves, but sometimes even that sly customer meets an untimely end; stoats very rarely, and even the wily rat is sometimes flattened, though no one would mourn his passing. Thrushes are slow movers, but you do not see so many thrushes killed by cars compared to blackbirds, and the smaller adult birds, the finches and titmice, are rarely caught by traffic. Yet the total of wild creatures killed on our roads in a year must run into many thousands, even millions. Some of these accidents are unavoidable, but in the majority of cases it only means a little care and vigilance, one can adjust one's speed when seeing a bird or beast in the way.

A Tragedy

Badgers are sometimes run over, but one hardly ever sees a fox by the roadside, in fact, I have never seen a fox killed by traffic. Rooks and crows, jays and magpies, never. When one considers that the latter species often descend to the roads to feed on rabbit carcases this is surprising, but then the jay, magpie and carrion crow tribe has ever been able to look after itself. Like everything else in life, it is usually the undesirables and rogues which get away with it. It is the innocents which pay the price.

Miniature Trees

My garden pool, which has been silent and deserted for over a fortnight since my moorhen cock was killed on the road, has new tenants. I think they must be two of the numerous young hatched last year, for they behave like immature birds. The cock arrived first, stealthily, for he believed the original owners were still in possession, and for a day or two he hung about, vanishing into the shrubberies should I appear out of the french windows. Also, he does not sleep on the pond, but roosts just below my bedroom window, in the very top of a dense beech hedge, squatting (if you please!) right on top of a sparrow's nest. Every morning he wakes me with various cheerful chirps and liquid conversations which give me pleasure.

His mate, a very small hen, arrived some days after, her appearance betrayed to me by much fanning of the male's white tail. On the second day he mounted her. This seemed to me to be a half-hearted attempt, possibly he will improve with practice, but he then confused her by crouching in front of her, inviting her to mount him! This, very properly, sent her into a rage and she pecked him violently.

Both lost their tempers, and they fought in the pond and on the lawn. Now she is minus her white tail. He has pulled it out!

One wonders sometimes at the tenacity of plants. The other day I was waiting in my car in a car park for a shopping daughter (every male knows what an interminable time we have to wait for the ladies on these occasions) and my attention was drawn to a vigorous tuft of green dandelion leaves growing out of a minute cranny of a stone wall close by the door handle of my car. There appeared to be no small crack or cranny anywhere else in the wall except at this place, half-way down, and there this plant was flourishing. I suppose it got its moisture from the rain seeping down the face of the stones, but where on earth could it find sustenance in that mass of cement and stone? How, too, did the seed get into the cranny – was it blown by the wind, or was it put there by a bird?

I was reminded of an ancient church at Culmstock in Devon, which I saw when I was making a caravan journey to the West Country for a book I was writing at that time. In the tall, square tower of this country church, growing apparently from the battlements, was quite a large yew tree about eight feet high. When I remarked upon this in the local pub, the landlord told me that it had been there many years, and it was quite a landmark and attraction for sightseers. Moreover it was culled from time to time and almost one hundredweight of wood had been taken from it.

How the yew seed ever got up there is something to conjure with; it may well have been from a bird dropping, a mistlethrush maybe, even a robin which had eaten the flesh of the berry and the kernel had fallen down into a crack of the masonry. Robins love eating yew berries. Curiously enough this tree does not seem to damage the tower in any way, and there was no thought of removing it. Indeed it was regarded as almost a sacred tree, and was as jealously guarded as are the chalk figures on the downs of the south country. They told me that some years before, the new incumbent to the living wanted to do away with the famous yew, and there was a tremendous outcry in the parish.

Five years since, when I was up in the north of Scotland in pursuit of my favourite quarry, the wild goose, I happened to make my way up rather a remote glen. In an old tumble-down stone wall I spied a wonderful true Bonzai yew! It was growing out of a crevice in the old wall, and I suppose it would not be more than 10 in long, but very bushy. I determined to secure this, and so worked away with my pocket knife to free the roots from the crack in the wall. I was only partially successful. When at last I drew it out I found I had cut the main root, but it still retained a great fan of fibrous roots which gave me hope. I brought it home and tended it carefully, but alas! it died in the end. Yews are tricky to move.

Among my many interests, I have a collection of genuine Japanese Bonzai. One, a magnificent miniature maple with a gnarled trunk is in its original Japanese pot and is my prize specimen. It must be nearly forty-six years old; its leaves are all in scale, and in the autumn it turns a wonderful glowing shade of rose and gold. Sometimes I have to trim the leaves, being careful not to cut the stalks, and this gives the tree a second leafing about midsummer, producing small neat leaves half the size.

These miniature trees, true Japanese Bonzai, take a lot of looking after. In summer they need water every day and do not like full sun. Since I was a small boy I have always been fascinated by Bonzai and I remember poring over the pictures in Harrods' catalogue, which my parents sent for each year, which showed very costly and ancient Bonzai trees for sale. One I remember was of a gnarled oak full of holes and crannies, a perfect ancient oak in miniature. The price was around £40. To try and grow your own Bonzai is hardly worthwhile, as they will not be perfect until they are at least forty or fifty years old; some Bonzai are centuries old.

At the beginning of May, I happened to be passing a flooded pasture near Oundle and saw a large bird stalking about among green plovers. Luckily I had my powerful glasses with me, and to my delight I saw it was a black-tailed godwit, the first of this species I had ever seen. It was filling itself with drowned worms. After a while it stood on one leg on a little grassy spit of land, and there it sat digesting what must have been a very heavy meal. This bird was obviously on passage. Next day it had gone and the floods had gone too.

I remember sling bar-tailed godwits in full breeding plumage in Holland just before the war. This was near Den Helder, the

Dutch naval base. They were conspicuous birds, the males with the golden brown neck and breasts. The black-tailed godwit has a more sombre plumage and is almost curlew-like at a distance, until you see the straight bill which, in actual fact, has a very slight tilt at the tip and has a distinctive pinkish base.

As far as I am aware, the black-tailed is a most uncommon wanderer, especially in the middle of England, though a couple of centuries ago it bred in the marshes of Norfolk. My bird was excessively shy, and when I got out of my car to get a better view it took swift wing and arrowed about the meadow, coming to rest again in the flood water. In flight the wings seemed pointed, and the flight was more delicate and swift compared to the curlew's.

One other interesting note, an immature crossbill was seen in the forest last month, which showed they had bred there, as I suspected.

SUMMER

Swift Mystery

On the morning of May 7 I saw the first swifts of summer, a band of fourteen coming from the south and heading north. Having seen an excellent film on the swift, I viewed these strange birds in a new light. That a winged creature could spend its whole life in the air, resting only in the breeding season, and then only briefly for nesting, seems to be quite extraordinary, almost unbelievable. For the swift to mate, gather nesting material, and to sleep on wings that are capable of clocking close on 100 mph must be unique in the animal kingdom, though the albatross runs it close. It is a wonder, too, that being so weakened by the horrible blood-sucking parasites which infest them (due to their grubby nesting habits), they manage to survive at all, especially when we consider the enormous stamina which is needed for their long transworld flights.

To sleep on the wing they must possess nature's automatic pilot, and sleep they must certainly do, at least the younger unmated birds during the nesting season. It has long been a mystery where these juveniles roost; as they certainly do not sleep in the nest with the parents of the infant broods, there can be no other explanation. And another thing – not for them the green and smiling countryside of June, but the great cities. They are real townies.

Some years back, when lying in a hospital bed, not sure whether I would ever again see the green fields, my one solace was to watch the swifts arrowing about over the chimney pots which I could see from my ward window. In those soft interminable June evenings I watched with envious eyes that twilight drama, the bands of slender sooty arrows, shooting and screaming about the mellow sky. The sight of them gave me renewed hope and optimism and, as it turned out, all my stupid gloomy thoughts were quite groundless, as such apprehensions usually are.

This reminds me of a fact not many may realise. It is that

when we are very young, and very old, the wonders of this marvellous world of nature (unspoiled by man) affect us most strongly. In early childhood the impact is more vivid because our senses of sight, hearing and smell, especially the latter, are more finely tuned, but as the years advance, when we reach that time which might be called the Indian Summer of our lives, the preciousness of the natural world seems to me at least to be greatly magnified.

But enough of these philosophical musings. With the summer reaching its most delightful period, this time before the fresh minted green has gone from leaf and grass, there is so much to write about and see. Even the wayside margins, which a few short weeks ago were without any leaf showing, just sodden bleached grass flattened by weeks of snow, have burgeoned forth as rapidly and profusely as a tundra in the Arctic spring. In only a square yard or so what a multitude of plants are there! Nettles, as yet neat and compact, all manner of grasses varying in shape and size, buttercups, dandelions, sorrels, clovers, Jack-by-the-Hedge, the hemlocks – the list is endless. I am glad that the craze for poisoning the waysides with weedkillers is no longer done to any wide extent (luckily it proved too costly). Before the grass cutters come along it is a pleasure to see these luxuriant road margins, which are at their most attractive now when the bedstraws, the Queen Anne's lace, are in flower.

Some time back I wrote in the press – or it may have been a broadcast talk– about the use of marginal sprays and how they disfigured the countryside apart from destroying wildlife. I was amused to receive a most abusive letter from some old Colonel Blimp, who no doubt had some interest in agricultural chemical shares, saying I had no business to write such nonsense, that spraying was the best way of making the road margins nice and tidy!

Two interesting things happened recently. One was a visit from a man who had a tame fox. It was found as a tiny cub, together with two others, trying to suckle from the dead mother which lay outside the earth. He took them home and reared them. Each has its own personality. The one he brought was the least shy of the litter, though, even so, it was very coy, hiding its head on its master's shoulder exactly like a shy child. It was in beautiful condition, with a gloss on its guard hairs which is a sign of tip-top condition in a fox or hound.

The other interesting thing was a letter from a lady who lives in Northumberland. I can do no better than quote her letter. She says: 'We were very interested in your article about the starlings.* This is a hill farm about 700 feet up. We have a gang of permanent resident starlings. They started to hatch and rear little birds about Christmas time. In spite of the awful winter they have carried on as though it was spring! In all we have a resident occupation of about twenty starlings and they all come and go through one small hole.'

Now this is one of the most extraordinary things I have ever heard. I know that house sparrows occasionally go to nest in winter, though I have never come across this myself, but I never knew starlings bred in winter. As far as I can ascertain this is the first recording of winter breeding, so students of ornithology should note this down.

Woodpigeon sometimes breed very late in the year; I have found squabs in the nest in late October, and of course we have the winter breeding species such as raven, crossbill and heron, all very early breeders, but hardly as early as Christmas.

It may well be that for some mysterious reason starlings are changing their breeding habits. As I have mentioned in previous articles, we never hear now the continual 'churring' of the starling flocks which was such a feature of early June in the Midland meadows, a sound I always associated with fields of golden buttercups and the sight of flocks of drab immature

see page 26

birds sinking down into those golden seas to become at once invisible.

It so happens that I write this by my Big Pond at the end of a regal summer's day. The air is heavy with the scent of two kinds of balsam poplar. I wish I knew more about trees – I believe the poplar family is a large one. One of my trees smells of oranges and honey, the other of honeycomb straight from the hive. It is an almost overpowering perfume which somehow attunes well with this still, cool hour, with the swallows dipping to drink. Those two poplars have grown from two slender wands which I cut some fifteen years ago. I brought them home and pushed them in. Now they are near eighty feet high, competing with my two Lombardy poplars. All the poplars are fast growers, surely the fastest of all our native trees. It is possible to have a wood of them in under fifteen years.

My vociferous frog has only lately ceased his interminable 'coaxing'. His efforts bore fruit I think, for I heard another, with an albeit feebler voice, answering one night from the Big Pond.

The Bowcase Stone

It was one of those lovely days just before the Jubilee that I went with a friend in search of the mysterious Bowcase Stone which lies buried in deep woodlands not far from Geddington Chase.

After the long cold spring there was that sudden rush of splendour. Every wayside was decorated with the exquisite white lace of the ladies' bedstraw, and every hawthorn hedge was snowed under with the speckled blossom which perfumed the air.

Cuckoos were calling and we saw the first orange tip, whose outer wings so cunningly match the delicate green and white tracery of the wayside weeds. Brimstones, too, were voyaging about seeking out mates, or the uncommon buckthorn bushes on which to lay their eggs. The only other British butterfly which has the same shaped wings as the brimstone is the swallowtail, which has the same curved upper wing. In a woodland ride brimstones seem to have their special beat, jogging along the whole length of a ride then returning. Yet it is not entirely a woodland species and may be seen rambling along the waysides.

Our way led across a stately parkland adjoining Fermyn Woods. All this part of Northamptonshire was once in the great forest of Rockingham, which was one of the largest Royal hunting forests in medieval times, and there is still a sense of bygone ages when one walks this haunted ground.

In this eastern side of Northamptonshire there are many great woods, many of them practically adjoining each other, and deer are plentiful, both fallow and the little humped-backed muntjac deer, which one rarely sees. Every forest ride is marked with the spoor of these wild deer, and in the autumn the grunting of the bucks is one of the features of the autumn scene.

Crossing the parklands of Fermyn Woods, where the horse trials are held each spring, one can see many venerable oaks which must date from Rockingham forest days, some hoary and stag-headed, full of holes and caverns, beloved of the owl and jackdaw. We passed a ruined farmhouse with its neglected orchard and about a little horse-pond martins were gathering mud for their nests.

The first week in June must surely be the cream of the year, but one needs the sun to bring out the full beauty of the fresh minted greens in grass and tree. My friend knew the way to the Bowcase Stone otherwise I should never have found it.

Entering the great woodlands by a small hunting gate we threaded a narrow path almost grown in by brier and thorn. It was a relief to come out of the hot sunlit field into the cool green shadowed path, a path seldom trodden by human feet, but more of a wild animals' runway, for the spoor of badger, deer and rabbit was clearly visible. Mounds of white hawthorn showed above our heads, lit by the sun, and the air was heavy with its scent.

In places we almost had to go on hands and knees to keep to the path but at last the bushes gave way to an open glade and there, half screened by blackthorn, was the Bowcase Stone. I made a sketch of it whilst my guide managed to clear away the encroaching thorns with a bill hook he had brought with him. Faint lettering is discernible upon it:

> *IN THIS PLAES*
> *GREW BOCASE TREE*
>
> *HERE STOOD*
> *BOCASE*
> *TREE*

The strange thing is that little is known about this stone. What is certain is that in the Middle Ages there grew at that spot a great oak, possibly where the agisters met at the Swain-mote which was held three times a year: fifteen days before midsummer, fifteen days after Michaelmas, and forty days after.

It must be remembered that Rockingham Forest was of great size. In the time of Edward I it stretched for thirty-three miles from Northampton to Stamford and was of an average breadth of eight miles. It was unusual in that special trees, called 'fox' trees, were presented to selected foresters for keeping down foxes and other vermin.

The Bocase Tree, however, was obviously not a 'fox' tree for those were felled for timber at the appointed time. From its name, Bocase, it would seem that it was also used as a stand for archery practice. The lettering on the stone, which is certainly fourteenth century, possibly earlier, suggests rustic spelling, i.e. 'place' is spelled 'plaes'. The stone is some four and a half feet high and leans over to the right in a large hollow, obviously the exact spot where the great tree once stood.

How I wished that, by some legerdemain, I could be transported back some 800 years and see the men gathered under the spreading branches of the oak which must have been an acorn at the time of Christ. Perhaps even Robin Hood knew the Bocase Tree, a fanciful thought and one to conjure with!

I know I felt an ancient mystery lay about that secret green hiding-place, and its moss-grown leaning stone, weary with the relentless passage of the years, sinking to its sleep.

The Old Barn

It was cool in the big barn, reputed to be the biggest in the county, but I take that with a pinch of chaff. The locals boast it is the biggest. They may be right. In front of me the big wooden doors were flung wide, in fact it must be some years since they were closed, judging by the nettles and docks growing just by the right-hand door post. I was studying the sounds of the great outside, chiefly the 'chirp chirp' of sparrows and the clucking of a mother hen who was scratching somewhere out of sight for her chicks. Now and again a swallow swept in above me in a graceful curve, as though on a swing, which took it right up into the dim rafters overhead whence came low intimate chucklings. He had a mate up there sitting on five rather long-shaped eggs covered with black speckles. Other swallows flashed by outside, singing as they flew. A swallow, when it is happy in the sun, sings as it flies for the very joy of life.

A gauzy gnat fountain was dancing out there in the sunlight. There was no breeze to sway the column which soared up and down as though pulled by invisible strings. From where I sat I looked across the stockyard to the corner of the farmhouse with the purple lilacs just coming into flower. It is the cream of the year when the lilacs and the golden rain laburnums are in full bloom. A few years back there were carts in the yard, and in this barn too, beautiful things which brought the harvest in from the fields, made as gracefully as Viking ships. I have ridden home in them often as a small boy.

Many people might think me bone idle, lying back here in the hay watching and listening. What a boring occupation for a grown man! But every moment can be savoured if you love the country as I do, the sight of the swallows sweeping by, the clucking of the hen with her chicks and the monotonous chirruping of sparrows. They have quite a different chirp in winter, though I have never seen this remarked upon. On frosty days they sit about before going to roost, uttering a single chirp which has a more musical timbre.

Now a strutting cockerel came in sight round the corner of the farm. The afternoon sun shone upon his shining armour and his beautiful bronze-greenish plumes reflected the sunlight. He stalked importantly across my line of vision and was hidden by the right-hand wooden barn door which was once painted (how long ago?) with blue paint.

Minutes passed. Then a rabble of sparrows came fighting over a hen. They came like a noisy mischievous soccer crowd of rowdies, scuffing in the dust, fighting and chattering, a frightful racket. They fought in the dust and then fled into the bushes, still fighting. No other British bird is so vulgar and unattractive and so full of mischief. Yet the little tree sparrows, which nest in my old apple trees at home, are sedate little birds who rarely quarrel; moreover their crowns are a beautiful colour like that of a ripe horse-chestnut and their white cheeks have a black beauty spot. For some reason they never seem to multiply and they do not mix so much with their vulgar cousins.

The sparrows gone, and the cockerel, and the hen and her chicks, a quietness fell upon that sunny stackyard outside the great high doors. Even the song of the swallows was muted. The gnats still danced. The shadow of the doors crept relentlessly across the threshold. Then came a sudden loud clarion cry of a cock pheasant 'karkoff!' There is a spinney of ash poles hard by the big barn, where long ago I shot the woodpigeon when they came to the poles to roost in the dead, dark, winter twilights.

A moment later I saw him. He came stalking out, a step at a time, his round fierce eye set in its red black-flecked skin, staring warily about him. There was stealth in every cautious forward step, in the turning of his eared head, the formidable hooked bone-coloured beak clearly visible. What on earth was he about, daring to venture into the intimate haunts of man on a hot summer afternoon?

Perhaps one of his numerous harem was sitting on eggs somewhere in the spinney. He stood like a statue, then suddenly put down his head and ran back out of sight. I saw the reason for this. The fat tortoise-shell farm cat, Mr Big, was stepping gravely across the yard. He was coming towards the barn, no doubt after the mice. But like the pheasant, he stopped now and again looking about him. The cat has so much of the wilderness in him; when alone, and away from humans, latent senses become alert. He came right up to the barn door before he saw me lying in the sweet-smelling hay. He stopped with one paw uplifted, then putting down his tail ran swiftly out of sight.

Now I turned away from the sunlit scene and looked up into the soft shadows overhead where the patient swallow sat upon her eggs high on a dim rafter. A white owl is reputed to roost in this barn but I have never seen her there. If she does roost there, what about the swallow family? It was a thing to speculate upon. A vixen will not touch rabbits in the warren close to where she has her earth, maybe the white owl does likewise. But on many a dusky eve I have seen her floating noiselessly about this stack-yard like a huge white moth.

High above I could see faint chinks of light showing through the Colley Weston tiles, those heavy stone tiles which roof many a barn and house in my part of the world, but which need stout timbers to support their great weight. In the far dark recesses I could make out the dim outlines of a ladder, and neatly piled stacks of fertiliser. No hessian sacks now, but horrid plastic things which are indestructible. There was also a grindstone, a roller with faded pink shafts, and a pile of baled straw which towered into the gloom of the roof.

I could not help thinking of all those far off harvest days when the corn was brought in through those tall doors and maybe even Harvest Home gatherings took place, when trestle tables were loaded with food and many a gallon of home-brewed ale went down thirsty throats and rustic songs shook the rafters. I do not know whether there was a term for these Harvest Home gatherings but in the fens they were called 'hawkeys' and in those remote flatlands 'hawkeys' may still take place.

Strange to say, some years ago, there lived in this barn a race of wild white mice. One of the men working on the farm once brought one to show me, which gave me the idea for a book for children called *Alexander*. I sent this white mouse to the London Zoo and they were interested enough to have it.

Albino wild mice are rare, I have never seen another. I have seen an albino swallow and that is rare. Partly albino blackbirds are not at all uncommon. I had one in the garden of my present house for three successive seasons. Harry Churchill, the keeper in the ITV film *The Shoot*, told me he once saw a white weasel, and for two summers I often saw a pure white sparrow close to Harry's cottage.

Some years ago, when I lived on the Warwickshire border, I shot a partially white jackdaw. It was such a beautiful bird I had it stuffed by Spicers of Leamington. White red squirrels sometimes occurred. Long ago, my old friend Geo Bazely the bird stuffer of Northampton, who did some work for me, had one brought to him by the then Lord Spencer's keeper, to stuff. Bazely said his Lordship was so angry at the shooting of this squirrel that he sacked the keeper!

Summer Solstice

I am intrigued by my spotted flycatchers. This is the first year at my present house when I have had them nesting and I rejoice to have them, especially as my swallows seem to be non-starters, at the moment anyway, though they have been flying in and out of the garage.

A flycatcher, a male, first appeared in late May, and was followed unobtrusively by his mate in early June. They have chosen to nest in the virginia creeper just by my bedroom window and the strange thing is I only see them in the early mornings. The male perches on the tip of a conifer, sallying out now and again to snap a fly as he keeps an eye on the nest, which is almost invisible from the ground. Soon it will be completely hidden as the leaves unfold still further.

During the day there is no sign of either bird; they seem excessively shy. There is something most satisfying to me to watch the little silver and white flycatcher perched on his conifer spray, his tail jerking in the manner of a redstart or a wagtail. There is something tropical and foreign about him, despite the fact that his colouring is so modest and drab. Perhaps, too, I like him so because he recalls summers long past and the time I found my first flycatcher's nest in a knot hole of an old apple tree in the Nutwalk at the place where I was born.

The Nutwalk, which may still be there, was a long line of hazels and snowberry bushes which lay alongside the old walled kitchen-garden, where I used to catch white butterflies as they floated about the long lavender hedges which my father had planted. I was attracted to the apple tree by the anxious alarm notes of the flycatchers. When I climbed up I found the little rosy eggs lying in their mossy cup in the knot hole.

The Nutwalk was a favourite place for other birds, perhaps because it was rarely visited save when the gardener tended the herbaceous border opposite. And what wonderful nuts they were, large cobs juicy and sweet. At one end of the Nutwalk was a grove of ilex trees where woodpigeon built every year and in a cranny of an ancient leaning laburnum, a robin made her nest every spring.

When the likelihood of invasion loomed in the last war my father dug a large pit at the top of the Nutwalk in which to bury the family silver and other valuables, for he was a methodical and imaginative man (the pit may still be there, filled with leaves).

I noticed the first dog roses open on June 18 and I was horrified to see elder in full bloom, an early date and such a reminder of how the year is marching on. Also there is that heavy darkened look about the woods and meadows, and wayside weeds are now four feet high in places.

The other evening I took my fly rod and visited a little brook not far from my home which has lately been stocked with trout. Rather rashly I paid £12 to join the club, but so far all I have seen has been waterhens. This stream is a pitiful thing compared to the most modern West Country chalk-stream, yet in itself it is beautiful and set in comparatively quiet sequestered meadows.

The evening was very hot with thunder in the air. I pushed my way through waist-high grass and nettles holding my rod high, a lovely little brook rod built for me by that most generous of fellows, Richard Walker, in the long ago. Some cattle were standing at a railed drinking place, a real Midland scene, the water up to their bellies to protect them from the gadflies which, so I was told by a farmer friend, will only lay their eggs on the legs of cattle and never on the body. The mud rolled away from their wet bellies like smoke; their mouths moved in unison, like the jaws of football managers watching a League match. Over the pools beetles gyrated, and a fat vole sat on his well-worn clay doorstop chewing a green sedge.

The little stream wound this way and that, sometimes straight between high banks of weeds, then sharply curving under arching alders which love to have their feet in water and are never happy away from it. At one spot the club had dammed the brook, forming a long deep pool presided over by a majestic oak whose lower belly bulged over the ochre water reflecting the wavering ripple patterns, where silver beetles revolved around each other like miniature dodgem cars.

It looked a likely spot to tempt a trout, but nothing was forthcoming, so I went on through flowery weeds to the next fishable pool which had been dammed with a grill and logs. This had been swept aside by a recent flood and no doubt most, if not all, of the stocked trout went with the flood, as they did on my own stream at home which I stocked with brownies one late May. A fortnight later came a record summer flood that soon dealt with my fish grill which must have finished up in the Nene.

A hot stillness lay about the fields; distant trees and woods were veiled in a strange muffled blue glaze. The old Masters used to get some such effect by glazing clear colour over the dry underpainting. Afar off a cuckoo was calling monotonously every four seconds. It was so distant I could barely hear the first note, only the second which somehow reminded me of a distant tolling bell.

Looking along the stream I could see the dancing gnats illuminated by the low sun, each minute insect surrounded by a halo of light. How I missed the cheerful bubbling of the whitethroats among the tall weeds and nettles, or the more musical ripple of the blacktop, though the latter prefers the woods. Here, the farmers' corn grew strong and unnaturally green with not a weed or poppy showing, food for the multitudes. I do not like the road we seem to be taking; the things that matter to us countrymen are being eroded slyly and by degrees as secretive as dropping tide.

I came to a shady, swampy place where ancient willows leaned and bright yellow wild iris flowered, a secretive haven full of marshy smells, the sort of place a moorhen would delight in. Sure enough, out of one half-submerged willow branch was the moorhen's nest, I could just glimpse the large stone-coloured eggs, with their handsome madder spots, reposing in the deep cup. Of the mother or father there was no sign, they must have seen or heard me coming afar off.

I thought that the hours of a long summer's day would pass gently here, where the tall yellow flags drooped and the moorhen sat upon her spotted eggs among the dappled shadows, and no man came. Here the greenfinches would come to drink and the larks, always thirsty birds, would come to sip the crinkling water, bills agape with heat up from hayfields. Curious to think how bare and bleak this oasis would be in midwinter, with the willows bare, the sedges and flags rotten and brown, and ice daggers in the stream.

I stalked that brook for some way looking for a rising fish but I never saw a sign of one, only weaving flies. The cows raised their simple faces to me as I passed, all with that wondering look, their square pink mouths working sideways as they chewed the cud. In hot weather they must dread the open field where the sun glares and no shade is to be found, their woolly ears shuttling to and fro to catch the sound of that dreaded low humming which tells of an agonising stab. Yet feed they must; they cannot stand all day under the cool alders with the water to protect them.

As the sun went down, a fiery pink which told of another hot day to come, I saw an aeroplane pass over, heading north. In actual fact the plane was so high I could not see it, only the golden plume it left behind in a ruled line which must have stretched for many miles in that rarefied atmosphere.

It had been a fruitless fishing jaunt as far as trout were concerned but there had been compensations. How can one describe those rich moist scents along the brookside, the massive jungles of nettle, dock, and sedge, the smells which were intensified by the cool evening? Mingled with those wild scents was the faint aroma of 'pond' water and wild water mint. I plucked some of the latter to go with a smoked Eye Brook trout which I had planned to have for supper.

Song to the Sun

I write this on a day of summer splendour, though when this is in print the reader may look on grey skies. No matter, 'this is the weather the cuckoo likes and so do I', as Masefield sang (or was it some other gifted bloke?).

The hawthorns are laden with white and red, the laburnum is in flower, and the wisteria on the walls of my circular house are promising fragrant cascades of bloom, whose scent, coming through the open windows of my bedroom, forms a fitting accompaniment to the twittering of my resident swallows who, each early hour soon after dawn, perch upon the telephone wire which I can see as I lie in bed. The male (for his wife is on eggs in my garage round the corner) sings so lustily that the slender antenna-like feathers of his tail tremble.

I like to lie and watch him and am lost in admiration at this great little globe-trotter who, not more than four months since, may have seen elephants, lions, and grunting buffalo. He sings to the early rising sun – let there be no nonsense speculating why he does so. There is no 'territory claiming' here, he sings because his tiny fragile frame is filled with a vast happiness and the glory of being alive. I can go along with that, though not perhaps with the great sudden surge of ecstasy I used to experience as a boy, when all life stretched before me.

I have a story about my swallows. To tell the truth, I am not at all sure that my present residential pair is that which first arrived in late April.

That pair worked diligently, building a nest high up in the dim shadows of the garage roof, at the very peak. A well-made nest it was, sturdy and strong, yet on no supporting beam. It was a thorough plasterer's job and hard as concrete, being of clay gathered from the stream close by. The hen began to sit, and for some days all went well. Each night when I put my car away the cock roosted on the bracket of an electric light bulb

110

just above the two main doors. When I shut and locked up for the night I passed not a foot below him and he never moved. I never bothered to switch off the light before I went in, but one night, thinking that the bright glare just under his little belly would disturb him, I turned off the switch in the house before putting the car to bed.

This was a disastrous mistake. He did not move when I put the car in, but when I came out of the garage, and my head passed within inches of him, he battered around in a panic for he must have thought I was a cat, an owl or a hunting rat.

Both birds flew off into the darkness. For a fortnight they did not show up at all, and the eggs grew cold and addled in the well-built nest. But now they, or another pair, are back and building on a beam. Again the male roosts on the lamp bracket, but I have learned my lesson, I do not turn out the light before putting the car away.

I have two interesting bird happenings which call for explanation. The first concerns a pair of robins, or rather two pairs of robins, which built in a shed belonging to a doctor friend of mine. Both nests were within a few feet of one another with the respective hens sitting on eggs. This is really a most unusual thing in the bird world for robins are pugnacious little so-and-sos and will not tolerate another male on their home ground, especially in their breeding area. However one day my doctor friend went out to the shed and found all the young of one of the nests lying dead upon the floor beneath. So the robin had lived up to his reputation and I have no doubt that the rival pair was responsible.

The other curious happening occurred in this same doctor's garden, a garden which he has planted with all manner of fine trees and shrubs, some of them uncommon varieties. There are more birds there than I have, many more, and many species: goldfinch, bullfinch, warblers, tits, and, of course, song thrushes and blackbirds.

He found the nest of a thrush which seemed unusually bulky and tall. The young lay dead below with their heads bitten off; either a cat or a squirrel was no doubt responsible. Puzzled by the unusual bulk of the nest he took it apart and found that the thrush had built on top of another nest which contained addled eggs. I have never come across this before and it is difficult to see why this had occurred. Had the first sitting of eggs been infertile? Had the thrush simply built its nest on the top of another family?

He has a grey squirrel in his garden and I have warned him that his nests will suffer. In the autumn he and his wife watched it burying nuts in the lawn. This spring they saw the little beast come back and run about the grass stopping at each spot where it had buried its nuts, digging them out and eating them. So the story of the squirrel who forgets where his nuts are buried is not true. They seem to be able to locate them as easily as an oyster-catcher extracts a lug worm from the mud.

Soon I expect my moorhen brood will have hatched; they are sitting on six eggs in a cleverly hidden nest within four feet of my sitting room window. I say 'they' for there is a definite changing of the guard every three hours or so. The sitting bird, cock or hen, will utter a certain-sounding 'cruik' and the partner comes hurrying over from the Big Pond higher up the lawn.

With the summer racing on, flowers, bushes, grass, weeds, are growing apace; I shall soon be seeing the first wild rose in the hedgerows and the crumbly ivory heads of the rank elder. The dandelions are almost over, their white clocks blown away on the wind.

Now here is something to notice next year when the dandelions have finished flowering. Along countless miles of hedgerows and waste lands before the seeds form the round silvery white 'clock' (that is, when the silvery white threads attached to the seeds are still encased like a folded umbrella) you will notice that most have been split open at the side and seed extracted.

This is done by sparrows, bullfinches, greenfinches, linnets, goldfinches and mice, for the seeds of the dandelion have a great attraction. Just as we look for the first tasty pea and bean crop, so the wild things enjoy their seasonal delights. The mice climb nimbly up the stalks, mostly at night, and during the day the bright finches come and reap their harvest.

I have two great Lombardy poplars in my garden, which I brought with me from my old home six miles distant. Originally they were planted in a large outdoor aviary and when they were about seven feet high I cut the tops off, as they were touching the roof. I never thought they would survive the move, but they did, and now they show no trace of being topped. They are tall graceful spires towering into the sky and in a gentle breeze the pale round leaves rustle and wag, making a sound like that of distant surf. But the Lombardy does not sing in the wind as does the black poplar, a lovely tree to my mind, which is forever whispering in the summer winds.

I watched my trees grow inch by inch. At first they barely topped my garage roof; now they have shot skywards. Poplars do not show signs of upward growth until midsummer. In spring until mid-June they put forth leaves and lesser growth, then they race upwards and continue to grow until mid-autumn and beyond.

Another of my favourite trees is the balsam poplar. In spring it fills my garden with a scent like warm honey and even in winter the very buds are fragrant if you rub them between thumb and finger. Some people dislike the scent. I love it. I associate it with the purring of the turtle doves, those exquisite little brown-backed doves which haunt the deep recesses of the woods.

My balsam poplar is a rooted bough I plucked in the Forest of Salcey one summer day long ago when I was looking for purple emperors. My purple emperor larvae I have brought through the winter are almost ready to pupate. In a fortnight's time I shall release them in a reserve to bring forth children of their own.

True Countrymen

The cornfield between my house and the forest is filling up, a beautiful level sea of green. This field, which I saw drilled and sown at the back end of the year, reminds me so much of a great lake. First there was the brown earth, then came a film of green over which the lapwings tossed and cried in the spring, then the slowly rising tide which flooded ever higher until the tops of clipped boundary hedges, like the banks of a pool, are on a level with the flood.

Now the great expanse is full, the tide has spent itself and soon that wide sea will be tawny in ripeness, brimming level with the hedges. The man who farms this land knows his job and deserves this harvest of his labours. Sometimes he flies over it in his plane and no doubt relishes his bird's eye view. He has drained the field with deep ditches, and where the water used to lie for weeks under the winter rains, now he can grow strong corn.

The hedges which were once ragged and wild he has clipped by machine so that now they are dense and thick, a harbour for the small birds, the finches and warblers; these alas, are now so few compared to the old days. At first I hated to see the hedge cutters at work, brutally slashing and trimming, but where this new method is carried out in a systematic fashion each year a fine dense barrier emerges. In some ways, I regret the passing of those huge, old thorn hedges, high enough for a magpie to build in, but in time they formed no true barrier to stock; all the dense growth went up above.

Such a clipped machine-cut hedge is more efficient than the cut and laid, though it may not look so natural as the latter. There are few men left like my old friend, 'Tubby' John, who is an expert hedger; there's many a 'crack' I've had with him in the dour days of winter and it is a joy to watch him at work with his billhook, a true countryman, and a sportsman too, whose marksmanship with the gun is better than that of many a grand

114

squire. Such a man, if put to work in a factory, or forced to live in a town, would pine away like a caged bird, of that I am sure.

I remember an old wildfowler friend in the north, with whom I used to shoot each winter, ambushing the greylags and the pinks on the shores of the firth, who fell ill at the end of his life and was taken to the local hospital. That terrible time he bore with fortitude, but in a letter to me he said he was pining and sick for the wild shore and the sight of the skeins coming in at dawn, and felt that life had nothing more for him.

Long before the last war I used to stay with him in his little cottage not far from the firth. Close by his back door there ran a deep burn which eventually ran into the firth half a mile away and up this there ran sea-trout, quite big fish, which Bob netted and caught, lovely silver creatures weighing four or five pounds. Looking at that narrow burn one would never believe that fish ran up it.

Many a time I have been out on the firth for the morning flight and come back empty handed, but Bob would appear with the bag on his back bulging with geese. He had one or two secret spots which could only be reached by dangerous paths and there was also a freshwater pool, well hidden, where he bagged teal and mallard. I discovered these secret places of Bob's after he had gone and, like him, reaped a good harvest of duck and geese. When last I was there I found a mob of bobble-hatted townie 'cowboys' armed with rifles and repeater guns surrounded by a litter of paper and beer bottles.

I am glad I knew this firth in its great days and was able, albeit for a short interval, to share the sport with my old friend Bob. He was no mean hand at bird-stuffing and painting too. He had a wonderful springer spaniel which was his constant companion. In his will he left this to my old fowling partner Major Oakey who, like Bob, is no more in this world. Nor did the dog survive long, perhaps like his old beloved master, he pined for the shore, and I do not think Oakey had him for more than a year.

The birds are silent now. I heard the cuckoo in May and during the heatwave in June when he called late into the evening, but now the old birds will be on their way, leaving the young to follow. What a strange thing is that hypnotic wheezing hunger cry of the young cuckoo!

I remember seeing one sitting on a croquet hoop on the lawn of my old home being fed by a pair of hedge sparrows, a robin and a wagtail. Which were the foster parents I do not know, birds seem unable to resist that strange cry.

Now is the time when the flies are beginning to be a nuisance. When I walk in the forest they follow in a humming crowd and you can only lose them by diving into the bushes. A sprig of elderflower is effective, I find, stuck in the side of my deerstalker, but at times even this fails. The strange thing is that last summer I was never bothered by the flies in the woods. They usually emerge after rain; a long dry spell seems to discourage them.

The city dweller, walking the concrete jungles, does not know what it is to be pursued by several hundred flies. In one Oxfordshire forest I know well, one can be assaulted by fearsome biting flies, those long-bodied grey flies which alight on neck or hand more gently than a feather and the first thing you know is a vicious bite. These horse flies can betray their arrival by a very deep hum, a most sinister sound. You find them only on very close, hot days in the ridings in the woods or by the side of rivers. I remember rowing with my father up the river Dart in Devon one hot summer afternoon and we were attacked by hordes of these horrible biting pests.

When walking in the woodland rides I smear various repellents on neck, wrists, face, and forehead, but some of them have such a nasty aroma I almost prefer the biting flies. In any case I have never found them much good. Once when camping by the side of the Esk in Scotland my brother and I were nearly demented by midges which descended on us in a grey veil. No fly repellent made will keep these little devils at bay; the only respite was to light a fire, pile damp grass upon it, and sit in the smoke. Smoke is the only thing which will drive away all insect pests and every evening we had to light our grass fire. No small wonder the deer leave the low ground for the high tops in summer.

In the sultry heats of these dog days you can see the cattle panic and run. The sinister humming of the warble flies sets them off and away they go, forsaking the cool elm shade. The fierce pain inflicted by these stinging flies is considerable, and when one comes to think of it the sharp, rigid, egg depositor must be akin to the doctor's needle, but many times more painful.

Talking of elms, I am shocked to see all over the Midlands the ravages of the elm disease. Our fine hedgerow elms stand stark and decaying all about the fields, winter trees in the midst of the bosky greens of the oaks and ashes, a sort of tree myxomatosis. It is a dreadful thing to think that our elms have gone, and are still going, for they were such a feature of our landscape, but I would rather the elm went than the oak.

One result I suppose of this elm disease is that the large tortoiseshell, which fed upon it in its larval stage, will finally become extinct, like the Barnwell Wold race of the large blue, and the large copper of the fens. And talking of butterflies reminds me that I would not be in the least surprised if there are still some undiscovered species of British butterflies, hitherto quite unknown, to be found in the remote moors and mountains of the highlands of Scotland. I am thinking of the Arran Brown, an insignificant little butterfly which has only been taken a few times in Scotland, once near Galashiels.

I have never forgotten my only sight of a milkweed butterfly in Norfolk. One August afternoon in hot sun I was going down a lane near Cromer when a milkweed floated over the hedge in front of me. It is a slow flier and for a few yards it flapped along in front of me and then departed over the hedge. I never saw it again.

And I am reminded of an old parson friend who was a great collector and expert on both butterflies and moths telling me that one hot day, when collecting between Kettering and North-ampton in Sywell Wood, which has since been felled, a Queen of Spain fritillary settled on the white handkerchief he had upon his head to keep off the flies. He made a pass at it with his net and missed!

Birds and their Young

In the middle of June my moorhen chicks started to hatch close by my sitting-room window. One single black chick the size of a walnut made a brief investigation of its brave new world and was quickly ushered back into the nest by a watchful father. It was the father which first gave an inkling of the birth of his first-born. He rushed about the garden in wild excitement, hurrying this way and that with nesting material which he handed to his wife. There is another wild father which shows this excitement when the young are hatching, and that is the cock partridge. Both species are admirable parents with a watchful eye on the newly born young.

Drama unfolded as the days went by. When all six eggs had hatched and the infants had left the nest, they were conducted over the rockery to the upper Big Pond. This journey was not without incident for the weaker babies; those which hatched last made heavy weather of negotiating the rockery, scrambling and falling about, to the great consternation of father. But all soon made the Big Pond, where mother had constructed a special day nursery in a clump of wild iris.

The brood spent their first day there, but as evening advanced the parents had the difficult task of taking their children back to the night nursery where they were born, as there was no proper nest on the Big Pond. The inevitable happened, some babies were good and went to bed, the others chose to linger on the Big Pond. There was much frantic rushing to and fro by both parents until at last the tiny black balls were put to bed.

I was amused to see the cock scaring off my big golden orfe who sometimes came swimming near the nest. It was driven off by vicious pecks and stabs, which show how moorhens realise the danger from big fish, for pike take many a baby chick of both moorhen and mallard.

There seemed to be a vast amount of food invisible to me

119

on the surface of the water for both parents swam swiftly about pecking off insects, water skaters and the like, and greenfly which fell off the willows. I could very readily see what dangers lurk in the wild for the newly hatched chicks of water birds. Time and again one of the babies would get lost trying to follow its brothers and sisters through the maze of grass and rocks which divide the two ponds.

They jumped and fell over backwards with legs frantically waving and if a carrion or rat had been around, or a cat, weasel, or stoat, they would have been easy meat. Being in an enclosed garden and guarded diligently, not only by the parents but by my trusty labrador, any roaming vermin would be in for a hot reception, cats included, though these rarely show their noses as they can smell dog and my labrador is a great cat chaser.

I was wondering why young moorhens have such bald heads. They do not get head feathers until a few weeks old, and young coots are the same. The yellow spot on the end of the parents' bills serves the same purpose as the red spot on the lower mandrill of the black-backed gull's bill; it acts as a guide for the youngster when it is being fed, for the baby moorhen does not open its bill and gape for the food to be put in, but takes it from the tip of the parent's bill. The morsel is held out very gently in front of the chick, which has to take it into its own bill. All the while the tiny flippers wave and wag.

Now the process of herding will shortly be coming to an end, though each night the whole family still retires to the nest below my sitting-room window – a fragrant nest it is too, for it is surrounded by a honeysuckle bower in full flower. They cannot be in much danger there save from a marauding rat and I have not seen one of those around for some while. The last one made a home under my labrador's kennel but I set a trap in his run and got him. He was as big as a half-grown rabbit.

Recently I had a letter from a man who has tried his hand at rearing many wild creatures. One story of a jay amused me greatly. He reared it from the nest and gave it full liberty just as I gave my pet rook the run of the place. This jay proved an absolute menace, pecking the ankles of lady visitors, using terrible language (which I can only surmise could be attributed to its master) and also raiding the washing lines of immediate neighbours. Eventually it became such a pest my friend decided to take it back to the wild where it originally came from.

He put it in a bag and motored to a wood some nine miles away. There he gave it a piece of bread. The habit of this bird was, that when it was given food, it would fly off with it to the nearest tree and there devour it at leisure. Away went the jay with his tit bit and my friend decamped. When he reached home the jay was there to meet him, as jaunty and cheeky as ever!

He eventually swopped the bird for a pair of close-ringed hawfinches which were put in an aviary with a pair of goldfinches. Hawfinches do not get on well with other birds in an aviary. One day he saw the cock hawfinch sidle up to the cock goldfinch, reach down and snap its leg with its powerful bill. The poor bird fell to the floor but my friend managed to put a splint on the leg. The hawfinches were then kept apart. Many years ago I had a pair of hawfinches in an outside aviary and the cock bird was a very handsome fellow. They nested behind a screen of privet, the nest being built on top of an old blackbird's nest. The hen hatched two young which the cock bird soon devoured. I suppose in the wild hawfinches, which are wily and retiring, have better habits. It is now of course very rightly protected and indeed it is very scarce in my county.

Not long since there was an ancient orchard just up the road from me, a paradise for birds, and I often thought that if hawfinches were anywhere in my neighbourhood I should find them there. In due time the orchard was felled for the trees were past bearing, leaning and crooked and clothed in lichen. The new owner brought me one day a dead hen hawfinch from his garden and also later told me that his cat had brought in a fledgling.

Whether they are still about in that locality I do not know, they have not been seen for the last year or two, but there is a thick coppice nearby full of old hawthorns and some lime trees near the house so they may still be about. Hawfinches like lime trees because of the numerous green caterpillars found on the leaves. It was in the garden of this same house close to the old orchard that I was shown a dormouse, the only one I have ever seen, that miniature squirrel-like mouse with its bushy tail and rufous coat who seems to have little fear of man.

Dormice, like the hawfinch, are lovers of old orchards. In Worcestershire and Hertfordshire in the great cherry and apple orchards, the hawfinches can still be found, and when the leaves come off the trees in late autumn the nests can be seen, built like doves' nests on horizontal boughs. I have only found the nest twice in my life, one in Warwickshire on the horizontal bough of a cedar, and one in Northamptonshire. This latter nest was built high up in a may tree, again on a lateral bough, and contained one egg.

In those days I was an avid egg collector and for some ten minutes I gloated over my prize, that largish oval egg with its smoky grey lines and spots. I debated whether to take it but decided it would not be fair on the bird and, full of righteous glow, I descended the tree intending to visit the nest again a few days later when I could take a couple of eggs for my collection.

In due course I climbed the tree. Something, a jay, jackdaw, magpie, or even some other small boy, had been there before me. The nest was empty! Even now I can recall the pang of real despair which I felt on feeling into that empty nest and realising the egg had gone.

The nip which a hawfinch can give you is as powerful and damaging as the nip of a parrot, for the immense bill can crack a hawthorn berry with ease. In flight it is a most arresting sight, for the white patches on the wing show as clearly as those on the magpie and the flight is dipping like that of the green woodpecker. It can well occur in provincial gardens and orchards but is seldom seen, for it goes about its business in the early morning before people are about and is possibly the most secretive of all our wild birds. Why this is so I cannot imagine, few people would recognise it in the field.

Goose Feast

On July 19 last the remaining Iris (purple emperor) females emerged, two remaining from two dozen females and five males which constituted my winter wild stock which I brought through for release.

One of the females emerged in the morning, the other just before 4 p.m. I missed the drama of both. True to its maddeningly mysterious character, I have never been on hand for this actual transformation. I had only been looking at one chrysalis a minute or two before and decided it was not dark enough; when I returned ten minutes later the butterfly was out and hanging from the empty case, its wings fully expanded, though as yet damp and slightly limp. An hour later the wings were dry; both insects were ready for transferring to the forest some ten miles distance from my house. I reached the glade, parked my car, and walked up the ride with the scent of meadowsweet in my nostrils, a scent I always associate with Iris-time in the woods.

The evening was windless and very warm with a hazy westering sun going down behind the oaks. In the glades the solemn pink spires of rosebay willow herb stood sentinel, such a favourite flower with me.

I let both females crawl out on to my hand, lovely creatures with the white markings on the upper wings almost a buttercup yellow. Then they took off into the oak tops.

I went back to the car. As I came up to it I saw, to my utter disbelief a magnificent male purple emperor flying round and round; it was actually bumping the windows! For some three minutes it did this and then darted away down the main ride. Now had the butterfly smelled the females which I had had in my car? This is the most likely explanation. Insects do find the opposite sex by scent and this is especially true among the moth family.

How the misty evening sunlight made a glory of those regal purple wings. It looked to me to be in perfect condition and was

124

probably newly hatched. But what a ruin lay all up my favourite ride where the woodcutters had singled out every visible sallow and laid them low, with what destruction to my wintering stock is hard to guess. The next few weeks will show; so far I have found only one egg on a sallow that had escaped the knife and axe.

Journeying to another part of the forest I came across a fellow naturalist, a keen bird man, who hailed me with the news he had just spotted the first male Iris he had ever seen; it had been flying round a settling on the road. To find it in such an unpromising part of the woods, which in that section is entirely composed of young fir trees, made me realise what Wanderers they are for usually they shun the coniferous forest and stay around the oak plantings.

He was amazed, as I had been, for he said it was a wonderful sight to see this large brilliant purple butterfly floating around so close. Even the male Iris is full of surprises, for it is only when the light falls at a certain angle to the scales on its wings that the brilliant incandescent purple shines forth. Sometimes it appears plain black and white.

This man told me he had ringed more than a dozen cross-bills at that spot only a short while before. They must breed in the firs for some young had been seen. It is a very early breeder going to nest soon after Christmas, and the nest is rarely found. During the long hard winter of 1978–79, crossbills must have been brooding during the long periods of frost and snow which did not ease from Christmas to the end of March. My garden pool was thick in ice from early January to April.

I wrote just now of the rosebay willow herb, a flower that half a century ago was by no means common in English forests and I was reminded of a wood near my old home, a dense little coppice of oak and ash which was a favourite haunt of mine. It was there I saw, for the first time, a grove of willow herb in full flower in a little clearing. There was something particularly impressive to come upon those marvellous rose-pink spires standing expectantly with a background of dark oaks hedging them round. It was a sight I have never forgotten though it has been such a familiar late summer flower since that time so long ago.

I must have been about ten or eleven at the time, and the memory is further reinforced by the fact I was attracted to the secret clearing by the continuous raucous cry of a young jay which had only just left the nest and could hardly fly. Young jays are as beautiful as their parents, with the same blue, black and white 'water marks' on their shoulders. The bird seemed to be intensely desirable. I tried to catch it as I wanted a jay for a pet but it managed to fly up into the oaks.

That wood had a large quiet pool beside it full of pike and teeming with roach and damsel dragonflies. Around its banks grew beds of water mint which had such a delicious smell when you trod upon them, a smell I always associated with the primrose-spotted jacks we sometimes managed to catch on live bait.

I grow this same water mint around my big garden pond and it makes the most delicious flavouring to boiled new potatoes. A whole bunch of it, put in a jar of clean water will continue to grow and provide flavouring to all your cooking where herbs are required. It has a more powerful smell than garden mint and is to my mind far superior. So next time you are beside the riverside, pluck a bunch, take it home and you will bless me.

On the warm evening now, in mid-summer, the whole surface of Big Pond is agitated by tiny rings which give the impression it is raining. But if I lie down with my face near the surface I see the rings are caused by hundreds and thousands of minute fry, fish hatched in the pond. These are infant roach and dace but as they grow the vast majority disappear. They are eaten by the bigger fish and water boatmen who are voracious devourers of tiny fish and will even attack and eat tadpoles.

The other day a fearful creature was seen crawling up the side of the stone seal which acts as a fountain. It was such a

monstrosity, it was enough to horrify a child. When it had drawn clear of the water a magical transformation occurred, akin to the hatching of an Iris in my cages. A handsome green Imperator dragonfly was revealed and before very long he was zooming about the pond.

Two friends from Yorkshire came for a recent weekend, fellow wildfowlers who are dedicated goose chasers. I dished up our last wild goose for them and it was, by general opinion 'out of this world' if you will forgive the cliché. It was so successful I now give the exact method of cooking. Three days before, it had been taken from the deep freeze to get really ripe. It was then placed in a covered tin, and the surprising large amount of goose blood which had come from it was poured over the breast which was smothered in bacon rashers. Garlic powder and a glass of port was poured over it, a few cloves stuck in the skin, and a peeled orange put in the belly, together with sage and onion stuffing mixed with pig's liver. It was then cooked in its covered tin for three hours at gas mark 1. Result, a triumph of gastronomy!

There was goose soup to start the feast, soup made from other goose relics of bygone feats. This disappeared with great speed and Jack, a mountainous Yorkshireman, drained the tureen to the last drop, and pronounced it champion!

Smell of Summer

I saw something recently which epitomised for me the very spirit of high summer, though if you asked me why this was so I would be unable to answer.

It was the sight of a portly woodpigeon, back view, flying up into a dense hedge of red may blossom. There was something about that fat grey rump, rather elongated, with banded tail spread, and with the flash of white epaulettes on the shoulders as it dived clumsily into the thick blossom, which gave a sense of the richness of full summer. No doubt at all that it had its nest there, a frail stick platform deep in the shadow of the tree, an absurd apology for a nest for such a plump bird. Why the squabs don't fall over the edge I cannot imagine, for there is no 'railing' to keep the infants in. Often when I have disturbed a sitting woodie off its nest it has kicked an egg over the edge in its haste.

I do not know if many naturalists and sportsmen realise that very soon the woodpigeon may be quite an uncommon species. Already I see that in Ireland they are talking of a close season. I do not suppose that the farmers will shed many tears if the pigeon departs from the agricultural scene, but for me it would be a tragedy, something to add to the elm disease, and the disappearance of frogs, wildflowers and butterflies.

I have a very soft spot for the woodie. It's a handsome creature with a neck which is shot with many colours, a lovely sheen like the sheen on a rook's wing but more colourful. I like that soothing voice too, so different from the 'moaning Minnies', the collared doves, which came to this country uninvited and which are vastly on the increase.

At this time of year, in high summer, only a matter of half-a-dozen years back, the forest opposite my house was full of a wonderful soothing murmur as hundreds of woodies cooed against each other in the mornings and evenings. Now I rarely hear one, and even the equally soothing note of the turtle-dove is heard far less frequently.

I do not know what the position is in other English counties but here, in the Midlands, there has been a magnificent display of blossom on the fruit trees. The old pear in my kitchen garden has been a mountain of white. Last year I only had one pear from it (Conference) but this year I should get a bumper crop. Pears are tricky things and tend to ripen altogether, so much so the taste of them, even the peerless Conference, begins to pall. And so the village benefits by free baskets of pears.

The hawthorns, too, have enjoyed a good flowering and their strangely rank sweet perfume hangs on the still air at evening. The hawthorns, the old straggly trees, are great favourites with me. Some live to a great age, several centuries. I remember they were a great feature of that lovely wild Wychwood Forest in Oxfordshire when I did a broadcast talk about it some years ago for the BBC, one of my *Series of Midland Forests*. Those hawthorns were very ragged and high, giving a strange sense of medieval times. I have seen similar thorns in Savernake growing in the wilder parts.

Out in the Midland meadows one often finds a solitary ancient thorn, probably left by the farmer as a shade tree for his cattle in the summer heats. The trunks of such trees are as hard as iron with their lower bark glossy and mirror-like with the rubbing of countless hairy hides.

For some reason the woodpigeon loves the hawthorn as a building site, the hawfinch also, building its ramshackle nest almost always on a horizontal bough, rarely, if ever, in a fork. In the thick Midland fox coverts the woodpigeon prefers the black-thorn. There are dense thickets in the forest near my home which even a sturdy foxhound cannot penetrate. It is in these thorny, impenetrable jungles that the deer harbour in the daylight hours, waiting for the quiet time when the nightjars begin to whirr their fairy spinning wheels, for we have nightjars still, though not many; it is more of a bird of the south country and the west. I always remember a Welsh gloaming in Pembrokeshire when, as I was returning across a bracken waste, the nightjars were cracking their wings all round my head.

There comes a day or two (no more) sometimes in late May or early June, when all the hawthorn and crab apples in the hedgerows are in full fresh bloom. For me this time represents the very peak of summer, the top of the flood tide. For a few hours the whole atmosphere of the countryside is full of a faint perfume drifting over the field, and then it is gone. The white petals scatter and fly, they rest on the grass like snow and form bands of white on the little horse ponds in the meadows. This white blossom might be likened to the bridal dress of the year, a white which is echoed in the chervil by the wayside, and the white stars of the water buttercup in the ponds and stream, and white horse chestnut.

A couple of years ago I was out walking in the woods and came upon a blossoming bush which was exactly like a hawthorn. Yet I knew it was far too early for the hawthorn blossom, for this was early April. I plucked a spray and smelt the florets and knew at once it was not may. This bush smelled of something long dead! I was puzzled by this and sent it up to Kew by the next post. They told me it was a very rare hybrid, indeed even they seemed puzzled by it, yet the leaves were exactly like that of the hawthorn. I have searched for that bush since but have been unable to find it.

At this time of year in my part of the country the fields of oilseed rape are in flower, deceiving the eye on the dullest day with a spurious glow suggesting sunlit fields. This yellow is an unpleasant colour, quite different from the rich gold of the buttercup fields I remember as a boy. These strident greenish yellow acres have, to my nose, a sort of animal smell; they are not at all fragrant. Yet there are two country smells which I delight in, the scent of bean fields in flower, and the scent of lime trees. The latter does not come until the last weeks of July, it is the last sweet scent of summer.

On a warm day you can stand under a flowering lime and hear the whole tree humming like a busy hive as the bees gather their nectar. I heard this same sound this year when my apple tree was in full bloom, the whole tree seemed to be singing as the poor bees, so starved of sun this spring, were making up for lost time.

You hear this deep humming also in late autumn just before the first frosts, when the ivy blossom is in flower, and the black-berry fruit and blossom attracts a host of insects apart from bees. Wasps and flies of all sorts and of many colours crowd to this last harvest. When the sun of late September shines full upon the hedgerow this hum is almost as loud as in summer. But do not let us talk of autumn! It will come upon us soon enough, for already we are nearly within spitting distance of August. This does not bear thinking of, much as I like the autumn and the thought of my old friends the wild geese who are, at this moment, busy with their young on some flowery tundra and cliff face.

In the Woods

There was a cock linnet feeding on the rose-red sorrel seeds up the lane to the forest. The colour of its upper breast matched that of the soft slender weed. In captivity it never gets this lovely tint and in full breeding kit the cock linnet is a beautiful finch, more gay than the redpoll. It was soon joined by two others, one a drab little hen. There were bees humming up in the limes whose scent is one of the most fragrant of late summer, the yellow flowers, hanging in clusters, were shaking under the combined assault of hundreds of bees. These come from the village, where one of the cottagers has a large apiary.

There was a bush of late dog rose by the forest gate, the flowers cascading down in a graceful fall to the little brook which drains all this forest area, a mere trickle now in which the finches bathe, but a turgid flood in the winter days; all these were signs of the passing summer.

I went through the broken gate into the riding where the numerous horses from a local livery stable had punched it full of holes, making walking uncomfortable. The sun was hot up the forest lane, but once within the woods it was deliciously cool. Not the faintest breath stirred the upper leaves of the oaks. The loosestrife stood tall, a forest of pink spires where bees and beetles were busy, but there was a great silence in the forest save for the humming of insects. Had I been walking here some thirty years since I would have seen the golden flash of silver-washed fritillaries patrolling the forest paths, the grasses would have been alive with meadow browns and ringlets, the vetches in the cracked clay path a basking place for small coppers.

Now, only a few shabby gatekeepers and ringlets bobbed about. The ringlet is a humble drab little insect reminding me of its counterpart in the bird world, the hedge sparrow, that mis-named retiring little bird of our garden shrubberies, whose brief and not unmusical song is one of the first to herald the spring.

As I walked up the main ride I heard a faint rustle in the grass on my left and to my astonishment I saw a woodcock, which immediately took wing. I have never before seen a woodcock in this forest in summertime, but I know they must breed there, for they do so in the great woods on the Ducal estate to the west.

The ride before me was banded with cool shadow, the oaks on my left were entirely in shade, but on the opposite side they were in full sun. I lay under a tree and looked upwards into the intricate mosaic of leaves above my head. Tiny caterpillars swung on invisible threads, harvest for the willow wrens and blackcaps, though these are scarce now. In the spring I did not hear one willow wren in this forest, whereas some years back the woods were full of them.

The only bird sound I could hear was the foolish moaning of the collared doves, not a single woodpigeon cooed. Time was when this forest was full of the cooing of the ring doves all summer through, a continual soothing chorus which lasted from dawn to evening.

But soon I did hear one of my favourite summer visitors, the 'purr purr' of the turtle dove. These beautiful little gentle doves, whose sharp jerky flight and white trimmed tail make them so easily identified, are more plentiful than the ring doves, and their numbers do not seem to have been thinned at all.

Looking up into that vast green canopy above me, with its millions of leaves, was like looking into the depths of a clear lake where water weeds show deep down like green jungles. Hover flies hung suspended in the cool air, darting at times from side to side. Other black flies circled around, tangling in a knot like flies in a quiet room, breaking away, and circling again.

Suddenly there came the clear tinkle of the blackcap's song. In the stillness of the woods it sounded strangely loud and echoing, almost like the voice of falling water. Refreshing it was to hear that clear song in such a hushed and silent world. Turning my eyes away from the canopy overhead I looked up the ride where the shadow bands crossed the sward and there saw a picture which made the long hot walk worth while. A fallow doe was standing at the edge of the brambles some fifty yards distant, her big ears spread. She was looking my way. She could not have seen me lying so low under the oaks and there was no breeze to take my scent to her. Yet she stood there like a statue, the very picture of alert wild grace, a true woodland being.

All down the centuries there have been wild deer in this part of the country, I sometimes fancy that some aura of medieval times still lingers here, where the kings of England chased the deer and boar, and the deep baying of their great hounds echoed through the glades. After standing quite still for some five minutes, she stepped delicately out into the riding. She had a half-grown calf at foot which was as black as coal. She walked across the ride with her child skipping in attendance, and was lost to view.

It is difficult to estimate the deer population of this area. Perhaps the forest ranger has a fair idea, for he shoots them from the high seats in season. Some of these adult fallow deer are almost black. Up to a year or so ago there was a pure white doe, but rumour has it that it has been poached. The surprising thing is that these deer sometimes wander a long way from the woods and do considerable damage to the farmers' corn. Last week my friend Bob showed me a dropped antler which he had found in a newly planted spinney on his land, and a fine antler it was too. The deer had been raiding a small plantation and had bitten off the top shoots. They came in the early morning and were never seen. No doubt as soon as the sun rises they are off back to the thickets, but Bob's land is a considerable distance from the forest.

There are some secret parts of these great woods where nobody ever goes, save myself and the creatures of the wild, where thickets of blackthorn are so dense that they are only negotiable by crawling on all fours. That is where the deer lie up in the heat of the day, that is where the gentle striped turtle doves build their frail stick platforms and where you can see their two bantam-sized eggs shining pinkly through the frail interlacing twigs.

There also the bullfinch builds, again a frail rootlet nest, and you can see the little velvet black head of the hen peeping anxiously over as she broods her smoky, woolly, newly-hatched chicks. There also the long-tailed tits secrete their cunningly woven purses of moss and lichen, with very often a gay cock's feather to decorate the front door, for the long-tailed tit has an artistic eye and an almost feminine flair for decoration.

These thickets are no proof against the marauding jay, whose round, merciless eye spies out the nesting finch and tit, nor are they proof against the agile wood mice who can climb like jungle monkeys to despoil the nest of eggs and naked young. The weasel too, and even the stoat, can climb up into that intricate network of spined twigs; there is no rock-hard safety anywhere in the wild.

Under these thickets and close crowding oaks there is no underwood, only cracked clay and perhaps a fern or two and moss; there is not enough light for weed growth, and hardly enough for the ferns, which are small and weakly. Sometimes I see there the spoor of the muntjac, the Japanese deer, curious little misshapen creatures like the Hunchback of Notre Dame, toothed like a vampire and with barrel bodies. Very occasionally I see them, mostly in the late evening, but usually it is only a very distant view at the end of some narrow corridor in the firs, for they seem to frequent the firs rather than the hardwoods.

I can find little joy walking in that part of the forest which is planted up with conifers. Beneath the thick, tasselled boughs the earth is soft with pine needles; nothing can grow, not even a fern or moss, only here and there one can see split cones where crossbills or grey squirrels have been feasting. The only birds which build there are the woodpigeons, collared doves, and jays, and one seldom hears any bird song. The blacktop shuns the firs, and so do the other warblers. But where the firs end and others have been planted, trees not yet five feet in height, and where the underbrush is thick, the nightjars build. In mid-June if I go in the late gloaming, 1 can hear the ghostly spinning-wheels whirring and humbling like the sound of elfin threshing-machines.

I have never found a nightjar's nest, though a friend found two young in the forest last year. When these hateful firs grow tall and shut out the light the nightjars will go too, and unless other open spaces are made in the rotation cutting it will be banished for good. Nightjars are not common in the Midlands, it is a western and southern bird, and though it likes woodlands it will not tolerate dense shade.

Emperor and Empress

There is a certain area of my favourite forest which is never visited from one year's end to another by anyone save myself; it is my own secret haunt. Only in the stark winter days may hounds pass through in pursuit of a fox, but they will be unaccompanied by horsemen. How can I describe this secret green courtyard in the forest as I saw it this afternoon? The air was heavy with the scent of meadow sweet, not a zephyr moved in the tops of the oaks, and the flies were a torment, following me in a humming cloud.

I pushed my way down a deer track where the grass was waist high, interspersed with brambles, willow herb, and teazel. The forest floor sloped downwards into a hollow. Here was a wide space hedged round with ancient oaks and a few bushes of sallow, most of it 'going back', for the sallow has a short life and, though a strong and fast grower, it seems to outlast its strength and the branches soon die back; I doubt if the life of a full-grown sallow tree lasts more than thirty years. But here in this magic place, where spires of rosebay willow herb stood sentinel, the whole essence of a late August afternoon seemed condensed.

I had journeyed there on my fly-tormented way to search (of course!) for the eggs of the purple emperor butterfly, for this secret clearing is its kingdom. For a number of years I collected their eggs from the big sallows, but now those trees have died off in their nether regions, although higher up they look in full growth and health. I speculated on how many of the coveted eggs were laid up there, far out of my reach. It is true the empress prefers the lower, more shady sprays but I have found eggs high up in a sallow and could only get to them by climbing.

I sat down among the rosebay and endeavoured to deal with the tormenting flies by a whisk of elder which flies detest. And before long my vigil was rewarded, for there appeared over the crown of an oak the floating gliding shape of Iris, that rare and elusive butterfly, the most mysterious of all our British race, a creature of surpassing beauty yet so seldom seen, even in woods where they are known to occur.

Its maddening habit of remaining for hours on end up in the oak crown, where it is far beyond the entomologist's net, is well known to collectors. It is, I believe, the laziest butterfly known, and like the pheasant will not fly unless it is forced to, either by sexual activity or disturbance by birds, which have been known to chase and catch purple emperors. Jays especially have been seen to do this, no doubt attracted by the black and white flicker of the wings. Yet the flight of Iris is perhaps the most striking of all our native species. It is a swift and powerful flight with many soaring glides around the oak crowns. At such times when the sun is shining one can see the pale membrane bands on the dark wings.

I had my powerful glasses with me and was delighted to see my female joined by two others, presumably males. Once she floated down to the top of a high sallow, perhaps to lay an egg, though the time was late. She was no doubt just enjoying herself a sort of Indian summer before her brief life came to an end.

The sun beat down out of a veiled sky which seemed to intensify the heat much as a tent will do, and in my ears was the continual droning of the flies. The pink spires of the rosebay were motionless, occasionally trembling when they were assaulted by honey-gathering bumble bees and other insects.

The oak leaves were dark but showing fresh tufts of reddish green which told, more than anything, how the summer was wearing away. In the hot bleached herbage beside me as I lay in the green shade of a big sallow, I saw the grass blades moving with numerous grasshoppers. This pleased me for grasshoppers, along with frogs and toads, and hosts of other creatures, have been killed by the farmers' sprays.

These purple emperors of mine (they really were mine, of my own stocking, for as far as I know Iris did not occur in this forest in recent years) were extremely active, chasing each other about, gliding and floating around the oak crowns far out of reach. I could well imagine the frustration of a greedy butterfly collector who would have loved to secure one of them for his 'cabinet', how he would have groaned with despair of ever catching one with a sweep of his long-handled net. Turtle doves crooned in the deep recesses of the forest, true bird of those quiet thickets and whose companions are the wild deer.

Flitting about among the grasses were numerous gatekeepers, a modest yet warmly flashed little butterfly whose wings, in a certain light seemed to glow. A few meadow browns were with them. How as a boy I used to try and catch them in my fingers! But they always flitted away and I thought they saw me coming out of the round eye on the outside wing. I do not know whether the painted eyes on the wings of butterflies and moths are any deterrent to hunting birds.

The eyes on the peacock's wings are most pronounced. Were the peacock a rare butterfly it would be prized even above the purple emperor for the collector's 'cabinet'. Yet it seems to survive, despite the fact that nettles are now killed by sprays, for the larvae feed on nettle, usually those that are new growth after the first crop has been scythed.

As I lay in the shade a brilliant blue butterfly went past, so blue that I wondered if it could be an adonis blue, but then that is a butterfly of the downlands of the south. Lying back in the grass and still keeping an eye on the promised appearance of my purple emperors, I could see the hover flies hanging motionless, or seemingly so, as though suspended by invisible threads. The hazy clouds had moved away. I could look up into the ocean of the sky, and across that blue backdrop a white line was drawn as if by a celestial finger. It was the vapour trail of an aeroplane, though the plane itself was so high it was invisible, save through my binoculars.

This forest holds a lot of fallow deer, the little muntjac also. These strange little horned and fanged deer are little bigger than hares and they have colonized most of the big Midland woods from Woburn. Not long since, I visited that fine naturalist Phil Drabble at his wonderful house in the midst of Bagot's Wood in Staffordshire where he has one hundred acres of wonderful oak forest.

To my mind it was the ideal home for a naturalist of his calibre. There is a large pool below the house and he has cut two rides through the wood so that he can watch his deer feeding from his windows. When we were there, there was a pure white fallow deer with the herd. In his wood he has a heronry; not many can boast of a heronry of their very own.

Drabble had a charming little muntjac deer which had been brought to him when a few days old. It had been reared on the bottle and was perfectly tame, running around with his dogs. In the wild woods one seldom sees them for they are most secretive creatures and, like my friends the purple emperors, they can exist in a wood without anybody knowing they are there.

As I lay under my sallow shade I thought of the life of these most secretive woodland sprites, and the fallow deer also. What a wonderful woodland life they lead, and though occasionally harried by poachers, they are seldom shot save by the appointed forestry 'Rifles' whose job it is to keep the numbers under control. From my house on still summer evenings, I can see the fallow deer emerge from the fringes of the forest and enter the cornfields.

A friend of mine, a big and very good farmer, planted a number of mountain ash trees on the borders of his fields and most of them were eaten by the fallow deer. For some reason they seem to prefer the foliage of the mountain ash to any other tree, and at times can do a considerable amount of damage both to crops and timber.

Grebes and Gremlins

The other day I went fishing. The chosen morning reminded me of autumn. As I was discussing mushrooms and smoked rashers (I am an advocate of a hearty breakfast, which usually consists of bacon, sausage, mushroom or tomato, with a fried egg to top it off) I saw a sad mist veiling Far Forest, and in truth, as I set out, there was an almost autumn stillness and mugginess in the air; I almost expected the scent of stubble burning.

This false picture was further reinforced when I reached the Eye Brook Reservoir, for there was a weed fire burning on the high ground to the north and its blue reek drifted over the unruffled waters towards us. But a lie was given to the autumn scene by the cuckoo's voice calling steadily and far from the wooded eastern shore, and many swifts arrowed about us, as they were to do all day through, sometimes scything past our ears when we were out in the boat on the still surface.

My fishing friend was already there when I arrived and we set about carting our clobber to the boat, handily drawn up within a few yards of the car, an excellent arrangement as it is no fun transporting two heavy 12-volt batteries and a weighty engine, apart from rods, nets, and waterproof clothing. Cocking an eye at the sky I decided to take my trusty Barbour coat but I had foolishly left my Barbour bags behind, taking instead my camouflage trousers which are not really rainproof.

I am one of those people who like to carry my rods in clips on the car roof, for this saves a deal of trouble when I arrive. My friend does not agree, preferring to spend ten minutes or more putting up his rod. I have a suspicion that some anglers find a delight in fiddling with their tackle and selecting various lures or flies; they make as much to-do about it as some men do with shaving. I'm afraid I regard this as a waste of time. I have a battered nymph on one rod and a nameless and worse-for-wear fly on the other.

But... to business. The leads were attached to the batteries and it was a case of 'all aboard the lugger and the fish are mine'. We slid silently from the jetty and butted out into a rising ripple which slapped a jolly chuckle under our prow. I was glad of the rising wind. The sky was sullen still, soon to be spitting rain.

We had not gone fifty yards from the jetty before my companion was into a fish, for we were cruising dead slow and casting was possible. As he was using a new rod he had made himself in the dark days of that dreadful winter, this seemed a good omen. The fish was a nice one-and-a-half pounder which fought sternly before it came to net.

Not long after, I was into another and this fish also played merry hell, jumping like a sea trout. This proved to be a better fish by a few ounces, and then we headed north for One Tree Bay where a solitary chestnut was in full flower that gloomy day, standing out as a landmark, opposite which I have had many a good fish.

The wind was now gathering strength and it began to rain in earnest. Before very long we were hit by a deluge, outrider no doubt of the torrents which flooded the west country later that day. Not a drop penetrated my Barbour, though soon my thighs felt decidedly damp and cold. This annoyed me, for I maintain that whether you are fishing or shooting, if you are rightly clad, you should never get wet. As for my pal at the other end of the boat, with no protection to his nether limbs, he was soon wet through.

But come rain, snow, hail and tempest we rode out the storm and then repaired to the east side and its fir wood to return some warmth to our limbs. At last, in mid-afternoon, the rain ceased and even the cuckoo found his voice again. But I was not deceived by the bland yellow of the distant oil seed rape fields which were making believe the sun was out; there was to be no more sun that day.

Back in One Tree Bay, Ivor had another fish and as we drifted on to the edge of the weeds my rod was almost torn from my hand (I had been holding it in idle fashion). It almost went overboard. The reel made an urgent scream, a sound which delights every angler's heart, as sweet as the sound of summer cuckoos and midnight nightingales. The rod point bowed until it touched the water. This was a fish and no mistake, one of the big brownies.

Such a one took the fly of another angling friend the week before when he was fishing at Rutland Water. Like me, he played it for a considerable time only to lose it by the boat.

My fish took me into the weeds down and deep and the tiny nymph hook came free with the accompaniment of two heavy groans. I had a tantalizing glimpse of a very broad spotted golden flank, and that is all I saw of him. By the way he pulled my rod point down he was a real good 'un. But . . . Fishermen's tales! Fishermen's tales! . . . yet there lies a subtle charm of angling, the unseen quarry, the possibility of size . . . that taut and nodding rod and line, that unseen strength fighting you deep down.

With the wind abating and to the accompaniment of more monotonous cuckoo bells tolling, we each had another fish apiece until the gremlins struck. These mischievous little creatures must have been busy with other piscators and had overlooked us in our little bay (I have a theory they are winged in the later stages, albeit invisible to us).

At any rate my rod somehow went overboard (no, I was not trolling) and as we had the engine going at low speed I looked back to see just the tip of the top joint sticking up like the mast of a wrecked schooner. A quick about turn was made and my companion managed to grasp the top ring ere it vanished forever in the depths.

Unbeknownst to me, Ivor, wrestling with a mass of looped cast and line in the bottom of the boat let the major contents of the reel drape over the side. This was seized upon by the outboard as voraciously as a pike seizes a roach bait. In next to no time all the contents of the reel were tightly round the propeller. So the engine had to be hauled inboard and the next half-hour spent in an intricate threading and weaving operation before the line was free, luckily undamaged.

I judged it wise to make for harbour before the gremlins took another swipe at us; anyway, the hour was late and more rain was coming down. All the same, the day had been successful and one of the trout I had for supper that night, frizzled in batter, was as pink as a salmon and tasted almost as good.

Now all this, you will say, was really a very ordinary day, yet such days are never ordinary to me. It isn't just the fishing, it is the feel of the wind, and varying sky, the ripple patterns, the swifts rushing past, their wings working more like propellors than wings for I noticed a circular motion to those slender sooty appendages. It was the sound of a distant cuckoo calling the sight of a great crested grebe sitting on her eggs in a remote swamp, of a mother coot with her rufous-headed young toiling among water plantains; what a multitude of things there are to see when one is fishing! Maybe it is because I have what many would say was an almost childlike interest in quite ordinary things which give me such great enjoyment.

At this time of summer when the countryside is mature with the may lately over, and now the dog roses, there is so much more to delight the eye. I suppose there are some people who treat fishing or shooting as a game like golf without the slightest interest in nature and their surroundings. They would not notice the curious smell of the oil rape fields, a smell which I can now define as that of newly tanned leather; they would not notice the dusky swifts shooting along just over the grey ripples, or the pattern those ripples make and how they flash blinding stars when the sun catches them.

Truly, I believe, there are some who go through this life being only half alive! I can only pity them. When re-reading what I have written it seems to savour of a certain amount of trumpet blowing. I do not mean it that way. It is only that I wish all men and women could realise what a truly wonderful world we live in, away from city streets, where there are no cuckoos calling, or dog roses flowering, and no soft winds of summer, which smell of the countless miles of grass and wild blossom they have blown over.

As the Days Pass

The other afternoon I was watching three sturdy labrador pups at play. One was chasing a ball which eventually fell into the lily pool and the pup, in full pursuit, was unable to check itself. In it went. The astonishment on its blunt little face was laughable. But it did not mind this new element, indeed it seemed to enjoy it, until it was hauled out by its loose little pelt and deposited on the warm grass. That particular character will make a good water dog one day.

Seeing these happy pups enjoying their ball game made me reflect that a ball seems to have a fascination for mankind as well. We strive mightily to smite balls into little holes, we pick up a ball and rush with it to touch lines, we kick balls into nets, toss them into nets, smite them with bats and sticks, poke them into pockets round a table, smite them *over* nets and not into them, we throw them against walls, we even catch them in nets and run with them. Perhaps it is because of their shape and the ease with which they travel over the ground or through the air which fascinates. No doubt it was a round object which gave mankind the idea of the wheel.

Whatever this has to do with the country scene I really don't know. So to business.

A man told me last week how he managed to save a little green plover chick on a busy main road. He saw the mother with two chicks following and had to brake hard to miss them. He got out of his car and carried one of the little mites to safety. He turned round to fetch the other, when some ruffian driving at speed ran over it and killed it.

There are many people, I fear the great majority, who will never slow down for any wild animal or bird on the road. Countless times this spring and summer I have slowed the car to spare young blackbirds, thrushes, and game birds from being run over, hedgehogs also, when driving at night. The mortality on our roads must run into millions each year and in many instances there is no need for it. It is true that I would not brake suddenly if I had traffic close behind, but I am talking of those cases where there is no following traffic within measurable distance, which gives one ample time for rescue.

Summer seems to be racing away at a headlong pace, giving one hardly time to savour its beauty. In the course of only a very few days the white blossom rusted on the hawthorn, the bluebells faded in the woods and now the elder is in full rich flower. I never remember such a summer for elder. The waysides and woods are decked with the flat plates of mealy creamy flowers which have such a strange wild perfume that some people dislike but I find attractive.

Lately, my way took me along a disused country lane between spacious quiet fields where white-collared woodpigeon were nodding in the clover, an odd bird or two, not big flocks, and shiny-skinned cattle grazed, with great contentedness. As I walked along, I heard the distant 'telephone' 'burr-burr' of a turtle dove. The sound came from a little copse of thick hawthorns, elder and oaks some hundred yards distant.

The day was close and windless, heavy with the scent of the elder. A great feeling of peace and quietness seemed to wrap me round. For once there was no sound of traffic, tractor, or bumbling plane, just the sleepy 'burr-burr' of the little striped dove in its thicket. I could picture this beautiful little bird (for it is the most graceful and attractive of all our pigeon family) and its rufous-striped black and white petticoats, sitting in the green gloom of that secret place where man must rarely go, unless it is a farmer in the autumn, seeking after an acorning pheasant.

The male would be crooning to his lady-love sitting on her frail raft of twigs, her round jewel of an eye ever on the alert. All around her the chequered sunlight filtered through the leaf canopy in spots and stars of golden light. No stay-at-home bird this, however. They are great travellers. Before the mists of autumn form and the oak leaves turn buff and brown she will be away with her mate and (if lucky) two offspring to the heated African scene, a change indeed to this green gloom of the coppice in the very centre of England.

Thinking on these matters I could not help picturing the great cities at that very moment, with their heated pavements and hurrying ant-like crowds. There would be no wild smell of elderflowers there and sunburnt grass, there would be the whiff of passing cigar smoke or those sudden wafts of cooking food which emanate from city steakhouses and other eating places, around midday. These smells pass unnoticed by city dwellers, they are so used to them, nor do they notice the continual fret of the traffic.

Yet here, on this narrow road, burning in the midday heat, there was no sound but that distant dove, no scent but the thick wild smell of the elder telling me that summer is past middle age. It is these rare moments, quite ordinary in themselves, which give your true countryman such delight; they are even more precious in this headlong restless life when it is so rare, even in the heart of the country, to find a time of quiet and peace and freedom from stress and noise. As the cities spread and population increases with such alarming speed. I believe that people are turning more and more to the 'country scene' and are maybe beginning to realise how truly precious is our countryside at all seasons of the year, especially at high summer, with its hayfields, dreaming woods, and bright streams.

I find myself always fascinated by remote corners of the countryside, those far-distant fields in grazing country where the hedges are high and thick and their little drinking ponds starred with water buttercup behind their palisades of reed mace. Such ponds are now few and far between, for the farmer fills them in for fear of infection.

In these remote pastures and coppices the year passes so peacefully. Even at harvest time, when other fields are being reaped amidst dust and clatter, these cattle and sheep pastures remain silent and undisturbed.

The mallard love the remote ponds in the fields. They rear their young there and haunt the ponds all year. The greatest threat to the ducklings are the carrion crows and at one time, here in the Midlands, the little owl. The latter is now very scarce. I saw one near Oundle last month sitting on a telephone wire, a favourite perch for these day-hunting owls.

Apart from the occasional visit from the farmer to see how his sheep and cattle are doing, these remote pastures are as lonely as any mountain top or desolate moor. The woodpigeon love them, for they can breed undisturbed in the tall unkempt hedges and hunt at leisure for buttercup roots down among the grass. The magpies also own this kingdom; their huge stick-balls of nests are lodged in the high thorns and nobody bothers them.

Seasonal Reflections

Already, though it is yet mid-August, I see the occasional signal fires rising into the still air of evening, pale columns of scented smoke which tells that there are still some farmers who choose to burn their straw. The trouble is that with the new short-straw crops which are grown these days, there is not the length for thatching. Barley straw can be used for cattle fodder, wheat straw is not suitable. Yet I am glad to learn that this stubble-burning is regarded by many as wasteful and in time the practice may die out. I hope so. Some damage is done by fire to the useful little weeds which form good winter fare for the brown partridge.

I doubt whether the brown partridge will ever recover from modern farming methods. The only sizable coveys I see are those north of the border. Strange to say, the Scots farmers and lairds do not value the brown partridge as a sporting bird as we do here in England. One farmer I talked to, when I was remarking on the fine big coveys I had seen on his land, remarked, 'Aye, but there's nathin' on 'em!' Pheasants are a different matter, and of course the red grouse, that king of all game birds to my way of thinking, both from the sporting angle, and on the table, is *the* Highland game.

A well-hung young grouse, hung until it is tinged with-green, roasted and well basted with a wine sauce, is the best of all, better than pheasant, wild duck, partridge or blackgame. One can almost taste the heather in the flavour (I might add it seldom graces my table).

Walked-up grouse are not difficult to shoot, indeed they are easier than walked-up partridge, and I prefer walking them up with a setter, like the old sportsmen of the Victorian era used to do. In early winter, before the snows, I have seen coveys of grouse feeding on stubble fields well below the heather line. That windblown cry, 'beck-go-beck! beck! brrr!' is a real voice of the moors, as much as the voice of the curlew.

Though summer days are still with us there is a sure sign that it will soon be autumn. The tortoiseshells are beginning to come into the house with a view to hibernation. They seek out dark corners of rooms near the ceiling; their favourite place of all is in the folds of curtains. Early to bed seems to be their habit and it is strange to think of them coming in when, outside, summer still rules the garden, and other butterflies are still lively and on the wing. They will not waken until next March when the first sun of spring sends them fluttering at the nearest window. They are shabby, tattered and sorry objects then, but still able to enjoy a few more days of life in the awakening year.

The arrival of these summer-weary butterflies is the real first hint of autumn even before the leaves have begun to burn. I cannot help experiencing a slight pang of sorrow in the knowledge that the sun is voyaging away from us into the awesome immensities of space.

It seems but yesterday that I was remarking on the lush wayside growth of bedstraws and other wayside weeds and grasses, which, in the summer of '79, were unusually tall, in some places eight feet high and more, the teazles reaching a height of nearer ten. Now all these fine lush stems and hollow rods, once green, hairy, and robust, are withered and brown. The wild sorrel leaves droop, rust red, the hemlocks are like- wise pale and brittle, the tide is falling, receding back into the earth.

I hardly heard a chiffchaff last spring, though I listened for it in the forest, and scarcely a single whitethroat bubbled its song from the machine-cut hedgerows. The loss of these summer friends continually nags me, for how I rejoiced to welcome them after winter's end! W. H. Hudson wrote his finest piece in *The Return of the Chiffchaff*, which is one of the most beautiful descriptions of nature and its effect on the mind of man ever written. Whenever I heard the first willow wren and the other spring migrants I had a wonderful feeling of peace and content-ment that all was well with the world. Now the lanes and woods

153

of the agricultural Midlands are silent in the spring, even the song thrushes and blackbirds seem subdued.

I wonder now whether those joyful springs I knew as a boy and young man will ever come again, and I am filled with a sadness which strikes deep. For these were the things which I treasured and looked for and which filled me with inexpressible joy at being alive.

A doctor friend, Roy Walker of Kettering, who is keenly interested in birds, tells me he watched a lesser spotted woodpecker pair nesting in a suburban garden not far from Kettering this spring. The nest was in an old apple tree and before the Lessers arrived, a green woodpecker had drilled a hole above theirs but, for some reason, decided not to go on with the job. The male Lesser appeared to leave most of the nest drilling to his wife.

This little woodpecker is extremely scarce in the Midlands and I have only seen it on one occasion. Few people realize how very small they are, little bigger than a house sparrow. They have the same gay black and white barrings as the greater spotted, and a flash of red as a contrast. Young woodpeckers, when they are about to leave the nest and are fully fledged, keep up a continual serpent-like hissing rattle which must often attract predators to the nesting site. But a predator such as a magpie, crow or jay can do very little about it. As soon as the young become alarmed they retire hastily down the hole.

This reminds me of what I was saying earlier about the sounds of spring. The loud, clear, clarion call of the green woodpecker was one of the most typical sounds of the English woodland, a sound one seldom hears in the Midlands today. I wonder very much whether this dreadful lack of bird song, and animal and butterfly life is as bad in the south, in Hampshire and Sussex, those two delectable counties which, with part of wooded Wiltshire, are perhaps the best counties in England for beauty and wild life.

The wryneck and shrike have gone from the Midlands and

so, strange to say, has the common bunting. One of the chief sights and sounds of a Midland summer was the sight of the stocky, drab, bunting sitting on the telephone wires uttering his wearisome, oft repeated, jingling song. It was once plentiful all over the Midlands and eastern counties. I associate that oft-repeated jingling song (which I have now almost forgotten) with the hot dusty highway and a lazy summer's day. The stolid drab bunting was a most cunning nest-builder. The nest was almost impossible to find in the mowing grass.

AUTUMN

Autumn Glory

Just as in those days of late February we get the first subtle hint of spring, when we hear at late evening the subdued, unmistakable warblings of the cock blackbird, a sound which instantly recalls the glory of summer gardens, so towards the end of August I feel a subtle change. Even though the sun is shining and the herbaceous border is gay with summer flowers, there comes a strange sudden chill in the wind.

Looking across from my house to the forest I see one of the large stubbles has even now gone under the plough and the silvery thistles are white and flying up the lane; happy time for the goldfinch broods, hatched in the cottage gardens and apple orchards of this parish, for the goldfinch likes to build near habitation, possibly because their nests are so often ravaged by jays and magpies. There is something of the insect in the goldfinch, in its appearance on the wing and the way it flies. They always remind me of black and yellow butterflies when I see them dip away from the thistle heads uttering that liquid musical twitter.

The young, before first moult, are drab little birds, almost sparrow-like save for the pretty canary yellow banded wings which show so vividly when they fly. Seen at close quarters the goldfinch is a diminutive creature compared to the chaffinch, bullfinch and greenfinch, its smallness perhaps accentuated by its very short stubby tail.

A friend's retriever once brought him a fledgling goldfinch in its mouth and delivered it to hand quite unharmed. He managed to rear the bird, a most difficult thing to do, for the young are almost impossible to rear even when fully fledged, possibly because, in the wild, they eat a lot of insects. This little goldfinch lived for fifteen years and was a great songster and most devoted to its rescuer. It always gave him a great welcome when he had been absent for long and I find the same with my little hen bullfinch which is now six years old and which I reared from the nest. If I have been out all day and return to the room where I keep my birds she is beside herself with joy, coming close to me so that my nose is almost in her warm flank feathers, puffing herself out, and singing a very low sweet song right in my ear.

Looking into that tiny brown eye which is the bright window of her spirit I feel a great tenderness towards this little being which I rescued, half-drowned, from the nest after a severe thunderstorm, a storm which had drowned her three companions. She had only blue quills showing when I found her, but she thrived under my care. Like a true female she gets put out if I do not trouble to talk to her and seems quite miserable when I am away. In the wild, bullfinches are not sociable birds in that they do not go about in bands like many of the finch family, indeed I would say they are the only species of finch which prefers a solitary existence, yet they are supposed to mate for life; one rarely sees a bullfinch on its own, husband and wife keep together all their lives.

Linnets and redpolls go about in companies, so do greenfinches, chaffinches and goldfinches, siskins also, and even the shy and secretive hawfinch, such a rare bird now in Britain, has been seen to flock on the Suffolk brecks. Crossbills also will keep company, though like the hawfinch they are uncommon in the Midlands and east of Britain. The male crossbill in full breeding kit is a most lovely bird, with the breast and flanks the colour of those wild rose 'pin cushions' one sees in the hedges. They breed in the forest near my home, where there are vast plantings of conifers. Young have been seen and ringed and I have seen the old birds. They are very early breeders, nesting soon after Christmas. Why this should be so must be one of the great puzzles to naturalists for the hen will brood and rear her young when snow is on the ground and the blizzards sweep through the forest lands. No doubt they find some shelter from the thick tasselled branches of the firs, which can keep out the whirling flakes almost as well as a roof. Even when the snow lies deep outside the woods there is but a faint powdering on the forest floor.

It seems but a short while ago that I was walking round my lawn at eleven o'clock at night revelling in the fragrance of the garden after a day of heat, catching great wafts of perfume from the honeysuckle hedge and a medley of those other delicious scents you get near water after the heat of the day.

Now, it is dark at eight and I have promised to deal with two wasps' nests in a neighbour's garden. I would not be doing this save for the fact that wasps have been round my emperor cages during the day. If one got into the muslin box it would wreak havoc with my larvae. The nest holes have been duly marked, I trust, with white spills of paper, and a can of petrol poured down each hole and ignited should do the trick. Wasps keep a couple of chaps on the postern door at night but these will be quickly dealt with.

Another quarrel I have with the wasp is that it is a bad-tempered creature, like some of the more dangerous strains of bee, and will sometimes attack you without any cause. At the same time it has its merits. The mother is a tireless and devoted worker. The queen after hibernation has to select her nesting site, dig the hole, and lay her eggs all unaided, and will toil on until the grubs hatch and the workers can lend a hand.

On a warm afternoon at August's end I saw, on my walk, a field of uncut wheat which was ripe for harvest. A golden light flooded the huge field giving me a sense of great richness and fulfilment, such as one experiences when looking at a fat apple orchard when the fruit is ripe and ready to be gathered. On one side of this golden field, filled as it was with this flood of ruddy light, was a hedge, tall and unkempt, in which grew a row of stately oaks. These, like the field, were burdened with many hundredweights of pale fruit which peeped out in clusters from

159

the dark green leaves. The oaks cast shadows on the wheat, cool grey shadows, and there was not the slightest breath of wind to move those uncountable millions of heavy cornheads. There was stillness, too, about this scene; a sense, if you like, of Nature's accomplishment of peace and tranquillity. So this field has been all summer long, from the time of the chiffchaff and the sowing of the seed corn.

There was a strange remoteness about it, dreaming away the summer hours in darkness and in light, giving shelter to countless wild creatures, partridges and pheasants, mice without number, hedgehogs, foxes, hares, rabbits and myriads of creeping things. Yet in a few short days from now that peace will be broken. I had heard the larks in the days of early spring, when I went that way, and the crying of the peewits as they dived and soared over the newly-sown field, the wheezy cry of the jugging partridges, and stern caw of the carrion crows, who love these ancient hedgerow oaks for nesting.

Very soon that peace will be no more. The great lumbering combine harvesters will come churning in through the open gate with their long drooping feeder arms rising like the necks and heads of metal giraffes; the iron-shod tracks will shake the good earth and the golden hours will be filled with the shuttling sounds of the knives and the shouts of the men as they try to make themselves heard above the tumult of machinery.

Soon after comes the plough, but before that, the stubble burning. If the wind is in the wrong direction the hedge will be in peril, if the farmer has not taken the trouble to plough round the headland. The brilliant darts of fire will lace the field and there will arise clouds of fragrant smoke which will rise into the still air to mingle with other countless stubble fires which burn for miles over the surrounding countryside.

When the stubble burning is over and the ploughs have gone the field can be at peace again. But then the sturdy oaks will be bare, their branches glistening in the cold rain, the winter winds will shrill in the bare twigs. The ploughed land will clog the feet of questing partridge and pheasant, the latter, if he walks long upon the sticky earth, will soon amass great balls on his feet making it difficult for him to become airborne in an emergency. The pheasant dislikes flying and would rather run upon the ground. Not for him the joy of the cruising swallow, like those I saw sweeping along in the late golden light a foot above the ripened corn, singing as they went.

The Little Pond

One hot afternoon in mid-September I had a phone call from a farmer friend who said he was finishing a field of oats and there might be some rabbits in it. I found the field, a new one for me, and when I arrived, the combine harvester was already a quarter done. How hot it was in that big field! I saw the clouds of dust blowing away from the rear of the yellow combine; when seen end-on it did not appear to be moving it was going so slowly, for, though serviceable enough, it was an old machine.

As there did not appear to be much doing at this early stage of operations I moved on down the side of a fence towards a small coppice at the far end. I thought I should find some shade there, both for myself and for Polar, my labrador, whose lungs were working like bellows. The perspiration system in dogs is a bit dodgy to my way of thinking; they cannot perspire through the skin as we can. I suppose Nature, ever wise, has some reason for this. Perhaps if they were able to do so then they would lack warmth in winter. It's a question I must ask my vet when next I see him.

When I reached the little copse, which was close to one end of the barley, I was brought up short in astonishment. For here, in an angle of three fields, was one of the most delightful field ponds I have ever come across. Do I hear heavy sighs and repressed groans from my readers? Surely I have written enough about my affection for field ponds? No matter. Here was a gem.

How can I ever describe the impact it made on me? First there was the element of surprise. From a distance there was no hint a pond could be there in that arid landscape where the heated air was a-shimmer over the standing corn. Then there was the revelation on coming round a corner of a hawthorn bush and seeing this noble little water set below me like a jewel. No more than half an acre in extent, but with a singularly beautiful dense background of mature sallow and thorns and, behind, fair-sized

oaks crowning a sloping hill. In shape it was like a banjo. I will
call it Banjo Pond. I viewed it through a palisade of dead thistles,
whose silvery tufts were gently lifting in the wind, and the tall
rank spires of willow herb.

Seen against the dark background of water, which was deep
and fathomless to the eye, the silvery thistle heads and pink
flowering spires of willow herb stood out like the flowers and
plants in a Dutch painting. Most of the water was free of weeds,
but in two places there was a bed of water plantain over which
dragonflies played and zoomed.

The reeds opposite, bright green sedge of an almost vitreous
green at the base, were reflected in the dark deep water, as were
the drab greens and browns of the summer-weary trees, all of
which were exactly the tint used by the early artists in water-
colours, who always made their trees rather a drab selection of
greys and browns, never bright greens as in nature. Even those
greatest watercolour painters of all time, Cotman and de Windt,
rarely used a bright green in their pictures.

On the right side of the pond there was an opening in the
trees. Through this at intervals came sudden breaths of air which
sent sheaves of sparkling ripples right across the dark centre of
the pond like flights of glittering sparks or silver birds. Then
the breeze faded and the water was still again and sleeping, a
beautiful dark olive green in colour, as it reflected the oaks and
sallows on the opposite shore.

Never a moment passed but the surface of this magical pool
was not changing, like the expressions on a face. Now and again
there came a strange and mysterious dart of breeze which carved
a swift curving V upon the surface, just as an engraver might cut
the polished surface of his plate with his burin. After a while,
as I stood quietly there, two moorhens came out at the far end
under the thick beds of sedge and brier and swam cautiously
about, pecking at the flat beds of water plantain. Turning to my
left I caught sight of a large insect far out over the hot stubble.

At first I thought it was a butterfly, but as it came swiftly nearer I saw it was a dragonfly. It came rushing in over the fence and swooped down over the pool, where it was joined by another which chased it about.

In the autumn dusks this little pond is a great haunt of the wild mallard, though I do not think the farmer shoots them as he is not keen on the gun. Later I talked to a man who told me he remembered putting up a vast cloud of duck from this pond one day when they were partridge-shooting on the next-door stubble. And indeed it was just the sort of quiet and lonely pool which mallard love to resort to, preferring such a haven to the broad river down in the valley.

The dry, hot, harvest wind was lifting the thistle-down from the rusty forest in front of me, and some of these gossamer balls rose like hot air balloons, some gracefully soaring away over the trees surrounding the pond, others, thrust by a down draught, skittling lightly over the water.

I could have stood there for hours watching the changing ripple patterns on the surface of that pond, marvelling at the variety of effects. Occasionally when a stronger breeze came out of the west, ripple ridges followed one upon the other like miniature breakers on the wide sea, breakers not large enough to toss the flimsiest fairy boat. Sometimes there would be a sudden burst of silver stars exploding outwards and instantly dying.

I was soon brought to my senses by the dull, bumbling, sound of the combine coming along the edge of the standing crop. But no rabbits showed their noses, only a hare which popped up briefly right in front of the whirling knives, and then dodged away out of range, a sight which galvanized Polar into a frenzy. But he was secured to the fence and sank down in baffled fury.

Though sport had been non-existent, those few afternoon hours on the sun-baked harvest field, with the dry sweet scent of the stubble in my nose and the magic of that little pond, meant that my time had been far from wasted.

Foreshore Mallard

Although this is the opening of the wildfowling season, I must confess that I never feel particularly stirred at this early date. Some of the mallard have not been flying very long and have not learnt wisdom (though by the end of next month they will have learnt the ways of the world and will be as wary as their parents) and the grey geese have yet to come.

Yet my mind goes back (I dare not think how many years) to when I was staying with an uncle in Dumfriesshire. Those evenings in early September (with the prospect of school looming on the near horizon) when my cousin and I set forth on our cycles laden with 12-bores and belts of ammo for Solway shore.

In those golden days there were no restrictions, no bothering with permits, the foreshore was ours for miles, and not another gunner in view, save perhaps a jersey-clad fisherman-fowler out on the edge of the merse. There was one particular spot we always visited, a point of land where a large burn joined the firth and six or seven whitewashed fishermen's cottages lined the bank. There was the enjoyment of the long slogging ride with the stocked harvest fields on either hand, the blackberries in the hedgerows, overall the warm silence of summer's end.

We left our cycles by the fishermen's houses and walked along the short clipped turf to the tide line, to where the big burn ran into the sea. Here large blocks of turf jutted out from the banks, half dislodged by the equinoctial tides; these made ideal ambushes. I remember the quiet of evening, the sound of children playing by the whitewashed cottages, the call of curlew and the hoarse hound-like baying of a wandering black-back.

Soon the golden plover came by in little trips, following the burn and very sporting shots they were. Redshank, too, came jerking by, their white wing bars showing. We shot these quite legitimate fowl which are as good as snipe on the table. We only shot for the pot, never at gulls, or the tiny waders whose breasts

166

were no larger than those of sparrows.

Sometimes there would be the splash of a sea-trout going up and a scattering of spray among the shallows and spotted shingle. When the sun had gone and lights came out in the distant cottage windows, then was the time to look towards the sea where the far off rustling murmur told of the making tide.

Not until the first star appeared (one moment unseen, then, miraculously, it was there) did the first mallard come, bound for the barley stubbles beyond the firth. How unattainable some of them appeared, flying in compact formations, high out of shot, their stuttering quacks coming down to us out of the night sky!

I remember the last time I went there in the early 1930s, I had my single 8-bore, and I shall always remember a mallard, a single bird coming in from the sea, and how I fired and saw it fall and heard the thump as it hit the terse, a beautiful drake mallard. A mallard is somehow such a satisfying trophy for the game bag, the deceptively fat boat-shaped body with its bright paddles, the glossy green purple-shot neck feathers, the good-humoured bill!

Let there be no nonsense about not relishing what one shoots. Your true wildfowler delights in serving up the result of his marksmanship. The other day an eminent writer on country matters said that wild geese were unfit to eat. What utter nonsense! He must have a bad cook or a lazy wife. Roasted gently for half an hour in a covered dish with plenty of fat bacon as a shroud, and stuffed with herbs, both greylag and pinkfeet are excellent eating. Sometimes I pour a glass of port over them about ten minutes before I take them from the oven.

I like to hang my geese for a fortnight but do not recommend my fowling pal Mac's recipe. He hangs his not for days and weeks, but *months*, so I am led to believe. Once, when he wrote to me telling me he had eaten a November goose in (I think) March, I told him that I would visit him in hospital when he was fit to receive visitors. But then, I tell Mac that he would eat his grandmother if she had feathers on, remembering Wentworth Day's old Essex shore-gunner's tale.

It may be that one of these evenings my friend Bob will give me a ring and suggest we try for a duck down on the water-meadows. I enjoy these early season waits when the white mists creep over the river pastures and the peewits call thinly in the dusk. My favourite spot is on a side stream or 'staunch', as I believe they term it in the Midlands. This is thickly grown with reeds and screened by willows. The deep green pools are covered with the flat leaves of the water-lilies. I stand by the stump of an ancient willow tree which forms a convenient butt.

I like to watch the clouds of swallows hawking and twittering, filled with that unease and anticipation for the long journey which lies before them. Down among the reeds a fish splashes and a moorhen complains loudly at my presence, for they have sharp eyes and my ambush does not deceive them. To left and right stretch the cleared stubbles, Bob's harvest safely gathered into his big barns, and over these the plovers wheel and cry, filled maybe with that same unease which affects the swallows.

Occasionally I hear the almost-greylag call of two fat domestic geese which live cosily upon the riverbank across the big meadow. These two geese arrived over a year ago. Nobody owns them, they live a wild, free, life and converse loudly together at the approach of evening, no doubt their spirits are moved by a strange mysterious unease, for now is the time their wild brethren are about to set out for these shores from many a lone tundra where winter is creeping on.

As the dusk begins to cloak the fields I see hares creep out from their forms: solitary creatures, children of the wind-blown grasslands and the red clover, where the larks run and sing, bedfellows of the partridges. They sit bolt upright and then tittup along with their curious rocking gait. Over the willows (still in full leaf with not a yellow sliver showing as yet) the midge fountains dance and sway.

A bundle rises from a distant river bend, a party of seven unwary mallard, quacking as they come. They are in easy range if one were below them, but these go wide of my willow and vanish up the river valley where the mists are now milky and thick. Here come a couple, following the same line, but when some 200 yards out they change course and come slap for my willow.

The first shot of the season, will it be successful? At my first shot they tower upwards, at my second I see one fall. There is a splash among the reeds and Polar bounds away. There is no hesitation when the old boy reaches the bank, he launches himself out as though from a diving board (the bank is high just there), there is a sloshing and splashing, and the tubular reeds of the true bullrush quiver and sway.

A moment's silence, then grunting and more sloshing, the reeds vibrate violently and Polar scrambles out with the dripping mallard in his mouth. It is a duck and not a drake, more's the pity, but it will eat as well as the other. So begins a new season's fowling. Yet these tranquil moments of evening by the riverside cannot be called real wildfowling, that I hope is in store for me in twelve weeks' time.

There will be no leaves on willows then, the swallows will have gone, these dreaming stubbles will be newly turned plough, and the water-lily pads will be rotten at the edges. And I shall not be here by the winter river but away and away in my beloved goose country, hearing yet again the first goose talk as the skeins awake and fly.

It is believed that as we grow older the zest and romance of wildfowling withers and dies. Not so with me. The pulses still quicken when the pale dawn breaks and I see the black lines, like beads in a string, outlined against a pale, cold sky. Duck will come first, they always do, but I remain silent and heron-still as they pass over, for it would not do to shoot before the geese come.

Sporting shots though these may be, it is hard remaining so inactive, especially when I shoot so few duck at home in the dull Midland pastures. Yet this is how mallard should be shot, not poor, tame creatures which have been reared and fed and then made to fly to waiting guns. Invariably such bewildered birds are reluctant to leave their home pond and circle again and again while their companions drop to the cannonade.

No, my friends! That is not wildfowling.

In the Colonel's Cover

It must be ten years and more since I last visited the Colonel's cover. A chance meeting with the owner led to my asking him if I might go one afternoon with my .22 rifle to knock over a rabbit or two. Now, ten years is a long stretch. I expected the cover to be greatly changed, for trees which were mere saplings when I was last there, would now be good-sized timber. The place attracts me powerfully, for it is set right away in a fold of an upland plateau, invisible from any lane.

The afternoon was full of sun and heat. Beside the dusty, rutted cart track which leads to the cover, rest harrow, moon daisies, knapweed, and scabious formed a band of colour, and round the knapweed heads tortoiseshell and brimstones were flickering, together with a marbled white or two, which is an uncommon butterfly in my district.

On either hand stretched golden corn ready for the reaper, and the air over the track in front of me trembled and rippled in the heat. At my heels, walking in my footsteps, was my labrador, Polar, blowing and panting like a steam kettle.

The track led over two fields which were gated, and it was not until I came to the crest of the slope that I saw the tops of the trees in the cover below me. I suppose it is no more than ten acres in extent and was planted initially as a fox cover for the Pytchley hounds; it is seldom they fail to find a fox there on far-off winter days.

The little hunting gate was ajar and as soon as I was out of the glare of the sun I smelled delicious scents of damp shady woodland, and the cloud of teasing flies, which had pestered me all along the lane, dispersed. Once inside the gate I stood and listened. Somewhere, wood pigeon were cooing and a turtle dove purring. The hazel underwood was starred with pale nuts which made me resolve to come again at nutting time, for none tastes so well as the wild wood variety.

In a wood I walk slowly and instinctively feel with my toe for any hidden stick. Under the canopy of oaks the sunlight filtered down, making coins of flight on the grassy path which I noted was marked with the recent spoor of keeper Roscommon's big, nailed boots. In the centre of the cover I came to a wide clearing full of the pink spires of flowering willow herb, a beautiful sight indeed with the sun behind them, and beyond the clearing, surprisingly, two enormous cedars of Lebanon which looked alien and quite out of place in such a wild remote cover.

Why they should have been planted there nobody knows. Last time I was in the Colonel's cover I had been pigeon shooting, for these cedars are wonderful sitty trees and at one time a sparrow-hawk built there annually. I remember in the twilight a nightjar was whirring and reeling, an uncommon bird in this part of the world.

The warm, still air in the clearing was gauzy with insects shuttling back and forth. A large green dragonfly was zooming hither and thither, hoverflies in thousands, and the occasional swift flash of a silver washed-fritillary.

A movement in the upper branches of an oak made me look more closely. I saw it was a grey squirrel, fair game for the .22 and I would be doing. Roscommon a good turn, for here was a customer for the gibbet if ever there was one! My chief dislike of these tree rats is that they take a large number of eggs and young of the woodland birds.

But it was no easy matter to get in a shot. He was leaping from bough to bough and shaking the leaves. At last I saw him outlined in a fork and I brought the rifle to my shoulder. Just as I took the first pressure he vanished behind the trunk. Maybe he had seen me. What happened next was something I have only seen once before. The squirrel ran to the end of an overhanging bough and leapt for another similar bough which hung over the opposite riding. I saw him clutch desperately at the leaves, but he had misjudged his leap. He fell with all four feet outspread, like a flying fox, to the path below. The actual impact (which was quite a thump) was hidden from me as it was screened by foxgloves and willow herb, but when I walked over there was no trace of the little aeronaut; he must have fallen sixty feet or more!

That was the only thing of interest I saw that afternoon in the Colonel's cover. I had a brief glimpse of a white scut bobbing into the bracken, but there were no rabbits out at evening feed on the outskirts of the cover. I learned afterwards that Roscommon had been long netting, so perhaps that was the reason. I hung about the clearing until the westering sun went behind the great black cedars, and with its going the insect life in the shadowed glade faded away.

Standing quite still on the woodland path I noticed that, though the hoverflies and dragon flies had gone, there was a continuous procession of gauzy insects crossing the path in front of me, some descending, others arising, and all following a straight course. Closer investigation revealed a lively wasps' nest at the side of the path. It appeared to be in an old ant hill and when Polar, inquisitive as always, thrust a nose among the brambles close by, the warrior wasps were alerted and came forth to do battle.

Polar fled, shaking his head and snapping his teeth. I think one had stung him on the muzzle. Yet how does old brock badger fare when he digs out a nest? Surely they must sting him on the muzzle or round the eyes for a wasp will usually make for the face of an animal, man or beast. Anyway, we both beat a hasty retreat, and I made a mental note to tell the keeper about it when next we met.

Rise of the 'Fall'

The ornamental cherry I can see from my bedroom window is showing three pale-pink, elongated leaves. These are like the grey hairs on an ageing man and tell of the progress of the year.

There is another sign I can see as I laze in bed and that is the swallows on the telephone wire. In early summer the male swallow, my garage tenant, sat there to welcome the dawn and to praise his gift of life. Now many others are ranged there like beads on a necklace. Most are young, the summer's harvest, and I fancy there is perhaps a little apprehension in their hunched juvenile shoulders, an excitement, suppressed maybe, mixed with great unease. They depart suddenly in a twittering mass, arrow about the sky above the village and return.

There are other signs of what our American brothers term the 'Fall'. There is at times a sort of reverent silence which descends softly upon field and forest. The trees are motionless, the village smoke rises straight and high, there is a smell of burning potato haulms from cottage plots and burning weeds from the Manor garden.

At evening the swallows and martins wheel about in great companies and as dusk falls they descend, almost when it is dark, to the reeds in the little river, those tall plumed reeds where the reed warblers love to build in the fresh days of June. Owls too are active and vociferous. There is a nice boy in the village who has a good knowledge of birds and he rescues those which fall by the wayside, sometimes maimed, or stricken with evil agricultural and garden sprays.

The other day on his wrist he showed me a female kestrel which chattered to me in friendly fashion and nibbled my finger. He found it lying below the nesting tree, with a twisted neck which he cunningly put in some sort of splint until it was healed. He also has a pair of tawny owls which dwell happily in a barrel in a large aviary behind his house. These owls call others in from the forest and their hootings are heard from afar. He also told me that it was not long since he saw a pair of long-eared owls perched on the hedge top, within yards of my garden. I knew we had long-eared owls in the forest though I have yet to see one, perhaps they were drawn to the village by the hootings of the tawnies.

Another sign of the fading year is the activity of my moorhen family. Way back at August's end they were trying their wings and diving, and as soon as they could fly the parents set about driving them away, all save one favoured child which remains unmolested. These actions on the part of both parents seem strange, yet it is a sensible law of nature that in the wild no pond can hold more than the basic family.

The chases are fierce and unrelenting. Should one of the youngsters dare to come back into the garden both parents put their heads down like charging bulls and go right at the erring child. Meanwhile the favoured one, which is possibly the last to hatch, sits quite unconcerned at the fracas. Its usual perch is on the sundial by the big pond where it sits and preens, and looks superior. It has not yet acquired the black plumage of the adult, but is almost as big as its parents. If last year is anything to go by it will stay until the spring.

Occasionally now in these autumn nights, when I go out into the garden on my 'visiting rounds', inspecting my caterpillar cages for earwigs and other noxious creatures, who dearly like a feast of larvae, I hear, high up among the stars, the signal cries of curlew and other less identifiable sky travellers. Sometimes, too, the 'peep peep' of golden plover and the wild notes of travelling waders.

How little can we guess at the busy skyways at this time of year, our summer migrants flying away and others coming in! If like an invisible spirit, we could ascend into that starlit immensity we would come upon those travellers on their migrating roads, swallows, martins (the swifts have gone long since), curlews, both stone and common, sandpipers and redshanks, and, of course, the geese.

Bramblings and finches of all kinds, fieldfares, redwings and woodcock soon to be coming in, what a host of travellers we should see and hear! The ghastly business, so prevalent across the Channel, of netting these migrants simply to provide morsels for fat foreign bellies enrages me. Some countries have said they will try and stop this ghastly, yearly massacre but France will not agree, and so the spring and autumn slaughter of the innocents will continue.

In the forest now I can hear the grunting bark of the bucks as they move about shaking the yellow leaves from the thickets of hazel and thorn under the spreading oaks. The fallow bucks do not care overmuch for the dark shadows of the conifers, it is the oaks and other hardwoods of their forebears where they love to roam, and in a good season wax fat on the acorn crop.

The little Japanese deer, misshapen little sprites of the forest, seem to keep to the deep darkness of the thick firs; strange to think they are such late arrivals on the scene as they were originally escapees from Woburn. Now they are almost as common as the fallow deer in the forests of central England.

Why is it that the roe is only found to north and south of us? The habitat in our mid-England counties is no different from that in the south. It would be nice to introduce them, though whether they would be welcome in state forests is open to doubt.

Indian Summer in Hammer Wood

I have often wondered why both fallow and red deer are sexually roused when autumn comes. One would have thought that spring would be the time, when the great tide of life is flowing back into the winter-weary land. Maybe it has something to do with the gestation period, and that it is best for the calves to be dropped when the danger of cold has passed.

Walking the other day in Hammer Wood, the fallow bucks were threshing and coughing in the dense thickets, that curious grunt which goes on continuously as the bucks move around, maddened no doubt by the flavour of ripe hinds which comes to them on the wind.

It is a sound which has been heard in this particular part of the world since medieval times, when gay-clad nobles and even kings rode forth to the chase. I should like to have lived through seventy or eighty years in, say, the thirteenth century. How rich the wild life then, how wild and beautiful the land, *how few people to enjoy it!*

As I walked along the main riding, I thought of these things. I do not suppose the peasants had much of a time of it, life would have been quite uncomfortable in winter, but I doubt if food would be scarce. I seem to think the 'upper crust' in those days did pretty well for themselves, as they do even today under far less attractive surroundings.

The red leaves of beech and hornbeam littered the ride, filling each rut mark, and here and there stood a tattered and bruised sallow sapling with its bark torn off and branches bent and broken.

These sallows are always selected by the bucks, I think to clean their antlers, or maybe it is pure sexual frustration. They do not seem to go for other trees, though some young oaks may suffer damage. Not only do they break the trees in autumn, but they eat the leaves.

Not long ago, in another county, I persuaded a titled land-owner, whose lady was very keen on butterflies, to plant some sallows, the variety *Caprea*, which is the favourite food plant of the rare and lovely purple emperor.

I went round the woods with the owners and indicated suitable places to plant the trees, way back in little clearings off the main ridings.

We had not catered for the wild deer. Practically all the two hundred-odd sallows we planted the following autumn were eaten by the fallow deer, for we had omitted to protect them! Though the purple emperor still occurs in those great woodlands, there are not enough sallows to support a larger colony.

In Hammer Wood, *Caprea* is plentiful, and it was joy for me to find infant larvae among the sallows at the end of August, though I suppose only one in ten will survive until the spring for ladybirds, feathered birds, such as wrens and warblers, spiders, and most dreaded enemy of all, the earwig, will dispose of the rest.

I remember many years ago releasing a purple emperor in a garden after bringing it through twelve months from egg to chrysalid and seeing it fly off over the lawn to be neatly caught and eaten by a spotted flycatcher which had its nest in the creeper of the house!

As I walked down the main ride of Hammer Wood, a few late brimstone butterflies were jigging about, and peacocks were abundant. If the peacock were as rare as the purple emperor, how sought after it would be!

The tall rods of the rose-bay willow herb were topped with silver wreaths, balls of thistledown, glinting in the late golden sunlight and lifting and dipping to the faint northerly breeze, which somehow tempered the warm sun with a reminder that old man winter was just round the corner.

Near the centre of the great wood, where rides converge and where rustic seats and tables are erected, a grand fallow buck stepped out into the centre of the ride with his head towards me, displaying a magnificent head. He was the chief roarer I had heard way back in the thickets. He stared at me and my dog and then, with an indignant grunt, bounded from sight to pursue his uneasy and noisy peregrinations.

Only the robins sang from the yellowing hazels, a song which has all the sadness of autumn in it, a wistful regretful reminder it seemed of summer gone. Soon these trees will be bare, as the relentless wheel of the world turns us away from the warmth and light, this incredibly beautiful space-ship of ours which most of us take for granted and even destroy so much of that beauty.

It will not be so long now before the pigeon flocks will be coming in at evening with set gliding wings. Shots will ring out on some winter days and the gold-mailed pheasants will fall. The snowflakes will wander between these oaks and the full moon will go riding over a frozen Hammer Wood. Yes indeed, it is a long time to the chiff-chaff!

September Sunshine

Last September, when I was staying for a few days in a little cottage in a Norfolk village some three miles from the sea, I witnessed an amusing thing. Opposite the cottage was a large village green, a very spacious affair, and nearby, under a spreading chestnut tree, was a duck pond on which swam about a dozen tame ducks.

One early morning I looked out of my bedroom window and saw the tame ducks busily waddling on the dewy green, no doubt gobbling up the early worms, and with them was a gathering of wild mallard which had obviously flown in from the nearby marshes. The drakes were wary, standing sentinel with their madder-coloured bosoms thrust forward and burnished heads held high.

When people started to move about and the mists of dawn began to disperse, the wild mallard left, flying away over the chimney pots. I do not suppose anybody else noticed these wild ducks or, if they did, were vaguely surprised that the resident duck-pond population had increased a hundredfold.

At that time of my visit, the middle of September, when we enjoyed some wonderful Indian-summer days, when the sun shone from morning to night, the telegraph wires in that little village were strung with swallows preparing to migrate. The long lines of them perching on the wires looked like clothes-pegs on a clothes line. The shape of the swallow (and martin, too, to a lesser extent) is very streamlined, shaped perhaps more like a wild-rose thorn, the tail and wings tapering upwards.

It brings to mind an act of an elder brother long ago when we were boys. There was a colony of swallows which built in one of our outhouses and, if I remember right, there was a colony of a dozen nests all along the whitewashed ledge of the barn. My brother took aim with his catapult and killed a hen swallow as she brooded her eggs. He never forgave himself and we all felt

180

very bad about it, even though we were only aged about ten or eleven at the time. Strange to say, the complete colony deserted that barn and never returned. I have often pondered on that really very strange fact. It was as though the swallows realised what had happened and never forgave us.

This elder brother was to become a great student and lover of birds, and when at his public school won all the natural history prizes, including Keartons' volume on *British Birds*, illustrated with Kearton's own photographs. He died while still at school of Bright's disease, which can now be cured, so I was told, by modern medicine.

The summer of 1979 brought a plague of wasps, and though the wasp toils harder than the honey bee, I cannot like the beast because of its bad temper. Have you ever noticed that even the face of a wasp looks angry with its waving feelers and strangely banded mask? Hornets we never see in my part of the world, and indeed the insect is far from common anywhere save in the New Forest.

I remember Mac in Norfolk had a hornet's nest in an old dovecot. Knowing how painful a wasp sting can be, the sting of a hornet must be akin to that of a scorpion. There, if you like, is an evil-looking creature, with its curled and hooked poison tail, tipped with a deadly thorn of agony. I was amazed to see on TV not long since that a race of immigrant scorpions survive happily in a certain coastal town in the south of Britain, though their sting is nothing like so severe as that of the scorpion of the East.

W. H. Hudson, the writer, was a great admirer of the hornet, as he was of the adder. In one of his books, I think *Hampshire Days*, he describes a mouse and a hornet disputing over a ripe plum. The hornet had the best of it.

Speaking of mice reminded me that now the wild mice are coming in from the fields into the houses, for we provide them with uninvited winter quarters. The other night when I was reading, I looked up to see a mouse running along the top of the curtain frill just above my pet bullfinches. In some ways I like mice, for they are pretty little creatures, but I do not like them near my birds. They mess in the seed and can even kill caged birds. So I seized a coal shovel and managed to despatch it with a deft backhander as it ran along the pelmet.

I have not been so lucky with a mole which has been plaguing me for some weeks now. He started operations by my pond, and I don't like the idea of the 'little gentleman in black velvet' burrowing about under my pond liner. So I set a mole trap in his run. Now, I have always considered myself a dab hand at mole-catching, but this particular character managed to foil all my efforts. Each morning I found the trap sprung and the run filled with new fine earth.

He then left the pond and started operations on my front lawn, raising his unsightly piles of fine earth all over the mown grass. Thinking my old trap was faulty, I bought a new one, but again he sprung the trap each day and filled the run with sifted earth. Now he has gone and good luck to him! I like moles. They do no harm unless it is to top-dress your lawns, and they devour a great weight of worms. I believe their love life is unusual, but we won't go into that.

As a boy I remember I had a regular mole 'trap line' and would visit it each day like any Canadian backwoodsman. I caught a great many and skinned them, pinning them out to dry on boards and curing them with alum. I eventually sold my consignment of skins to a wealthy lady who forgot to pay me the sixpence a skin, but in the end I claimed my cash, something in the region of three pounds or so, which to me seemed a fortune. I spent it on cartridges for my fourten; in those days you could get a lot of cartridges for three pounds.

The farmers were only too glad to have their fields freed of moles, though I can't see that the little creatures did the pastures any harm. Sometimes cattle would kick the traps over or perhaps even foxes would push them about, though I do not think foxes relish mole-meat as much as mice. No cat will eat one and I noticed when I skinned them that they had a peculiar fishy smell, which perhaps is why cats object to them.

Moles work to a set time-table. An old gardener of ours would always catch one by waiting by the run at a certain time which was, I think, about 3 p.m. and thence would spear it on his garden fork when he saw the heaving soil.

Harker's Brook

Like so many names of fields and streams, nobody can tell me how my brook became known as Harker's Brook. It rises, so I am told, near a farm up in a fold of the hills. I really must go there one day. But wait! Would this be wise? No! I prefer to join it in its early youth, where it flows from outside the village and wanders away down the shallow valley between ancient leaning willows.

Like all Midland streams it lacks that clarity of southern waters. In hot weather the cattle are always stirring up the muddy bottom, the particles roll away like clouds, or sand-coloured smoke. A child could jump across it at midsummer but the winter and spring floods can turn the little valley into a succession of lakes and rivulets, a magical transformation.

I always begin my walk down a sloping track to the little bridge, a small affair of iron and timber, strong enough to take a tractor's weight at harvest time. On one side of the bridge it falls in a miniature torrent into a circular pool which is fringed with water forget-me-not and sedges. In the old days I used to find frog spawn there and hear them croaking in the spring.

I have cast envious eyes on Harker's Brook at this point, for the rounded shoulders of the hills come gently down on either side and it only needs a day's work with a bulldozer and some stout timbers, to form a dam which could transform the meadow above into a shining shallow lake. I have gauged exactly to where the water would flood back: the spot where two huge willows grow one on either side of the tiny stream. But there would be no money in that for the farmer who owns the field.

Below the bridge, the stream begins a series of loops and bends which resemble the pieces of a jigsaw puzzle, turning back upon itself many times in the most delightful manner. Here there is an ancient oak whose lower belly is awash, even in the driest season.

184

On a summer's afternoon, the twinkling stream flowing about the great buttress of bark makes waving luminous ripple-patterns on the twisted roots.

Beyond this, the stream suddenly blossoms into quite a large cattle drink now fenced in by wire and posts. Every summer there seem to be wasps' nests there in a raw red bank. The wasps, when they need wood for the nests, work away with patient concentration at the old fence posts, chewing little grooves in the silvery weathered wood.

Here, too, I have often surprised a kingfisher, for the little pond is a great place for minnows and sticklebacks which can be caught and beaten insensible on top of the fence posts. That brilliant blue jewel is such a strangely tropical being to see in a cosy English meadow. A snipe or two is always there, seeming to spring suddenly from under one's feet like something out of a conjuror's box; in winter the little jack snipe also.

Lower down the winding brook some thirty yards or so, there is a very ancient thorn tree whose leaning trunk seems to be entwined about itself, the bark glossy with the rubbing of countless hairy hides. This autumn when I went that way it was a mass of tapestry-red berries. What a sight it must have been in early June when the snow-white blossom was out.

Two fields on (a sheltered place for lambing in the spring), I come to the wild forsaken fields which are unsuitable for corn because of winter flooding.

Here I find a sense of loneliness and peace. I cannot believe that man comes here often, it is too far from the nearest road. The hedges are high, really old hawthorns, hedges which have not been laid for half a century, maybe. Harvesting may go on higher up the hill with all the bustle and vibration of the lurching combine harvesters and growling tractors.

This is the kingdom of lark, green plover and partridge, and maybe acorning pheasants, their coats gleaming like golden armour in the low October sun.

185

Hares, too, frequent these fields, and the shy mallards who, like me, delight in following the brook and seek out all its bends and corners.

In high summer the grass is lush and green; yellow flags and lady's smocks line the water's edge and in one place grows a lovely clump of flowering rush which, like the kingfisher, seems strangely exotic when its pink umbrella is in full flower.

It is walking in these remote pastures which I like best of all. Even now (when summer is done, and all the wonderful array of grass, and flower, tree and hedge, are rusting, weary and shabby) even at this late hour there is a wonderful colour running in the solitary field maples, and the crab trees are laden with fruit which fall at intervals into the stream with a 'plop' like that of a diving water vole.

There is a faint reek in the air from burning stubble fires as mile after mile, in all directions, the incense clouds of smoke ascend into the still air. And when at last October turns to winter and the flags in the stream lie rotting and brown, and the field-fares and pigeons have stripped the hawthorn berries from my leaning tree, even an idle man like myself will not walk those lonely fields The wild mallards will have the place to themselves and the hares will go loping through the dusk.

East Anglian Landscape

A visit to my old friend Mac in Norfolk recently brought back so many memories. I have a recollection of a strange happening towards the end of a shoot last time I was there. We were beating out the shrubberies near the hall. I shot a woodcock which fell over a wall into one of Mac's pig pens, for at that time he was a well known breeder of pigs in Norfolk which were always kept in an immaculate state of cleanliness. I seem to remember that particular pen happened to be empty and the woodcock was retrieved, much to my relief.

The other day on a beautifully warm Indian-summer afternoon, Mac took me round his marshes where both bittern and crested tit breed, and where the lovely swallowtail is not uncommon in season. I looked across the vast reed beds, whose polished stems reflected the warm sun, and whose feathery heads seemed to be lit from within by the low autumn golden light. Far in the distance was the ruin of an old drainage mill, a favourite perching place for harriers (and, once, an osprey), and where long ago I camped with a friend, Bill Humpheries, when I was doing a talk on Norfolk for the BBC. A few late swallows were hawking over the reeds and there was a great sense of summer's end.

We had with us corn for the mallard which we scattered round the shallow margins of a flight pool. Feathers and droppings showed that it had been visited at night. I remember some grand duck flights there long ago, for Mac has placed cleverly constructed hides around the pond which are now grown up with living willows. What a paradise this place is for the sportsman as well as the naturalist, with its wealth of birds and insect life, only matched by Phil Drabble's place in Needwood Forest where daughter Angela and I had the privilege of lunching, one beautiful day in June 1979.

As we left Mac's place in the early evening I observed in the narrow track a fat toad right in the middle of the road. I had to swerve to avoid it, the first toad I have seen for more than thirty years. I took it up and put it under my driving seat. The following morning when I reached home I looked all over the car for my fat friend but there was no sign save a small 'toad turd' right in the centre of my driving seat, though how he climbed up there I could not hazard a guess. I eventually found him inside the leg of my Gamefair trousers which were rolled up in the boot of the shooting brake.

I took him reverently to a ferny cool corner by my smaller garden pond and saw him crawl away into cover.

Professor Hoskins's fine series of English counties which I have enjoyed on TV did a specially fine job of Norfolk; he really got the spirit of the place as he did on the Weald of Sussex which I always think is the loveliest part of Britain.

My moorhen, alas, has been absent without leave for over a fortnight now. The last time I saw it, it was being stalked by a white cat. The brutes will come into my garden despite the fact I discourage them in a variety of ways, one being to set Polar on them. I distrust cats. I consider them selfish creatures and very sly. At the same time they can be a great comfort to old ladies, preferably spinsters. I doubt whether a cat shows you very much affection; Kipling was so right when he told the story of the cat that walked by itself. They have some saving graces: they are cleaner than dogs; they are great hunters, as must all be who like to walk alone, as I do on many occasions.

Returning from Norfolk across the fens, that land of massive skies and huge fields which, even in the driest summer, have the colour of dark chocolate, I saw a marsh harrier flying away from the road, that unmistakable buzzard-like shape with the long tail and pale rump, a bird I have not seen for many years, the last being at Mac's fen in Norfolk, perching if I remember aright, on the ruined drainage mill.

One does not realise what a flat land Norfolk is, because of the woods. It gives the impression of a bosky rolling countryside whereas, in reality, it is as flat as the fens. People who have lived all their lives in the fens and have been born there are never happy in hilly wooded country, they feel shut in and stifled. And I, who was born in the wooded Midlands, would be miserable in that huge flat landscape, where the heat beats down in summer without any welcome shade, and where the icy winds blow in winter in unrestrained fury.

Travelling along those ruler-straight roads (which must be purgatory for a walking man) one sees at intervals a far solitary willow clump or cluster of poplars standing out in the vast fields like becalmed sailing ships. These solitary trees grow in the dyke sides or in angles of a dyke, never in the centre of the fields where they would interfere with ploughing, for in reality this is really a giant 'food factory' landscape.

There are few thickly reeded dykes such as you get in Somerset to attract rare birds like the rare marsh warblers and rarer crakes, nor are these drains spangled with waterplants as they are in Somerset.

The flat West Country fenlands of Sedgemoor are quite different, there one finds great groves and stands of willow for basket weaving and the flat fields are fine for grazing stock. There is moreover the distant promise of hills and wood and even a hint of the nearness of the western sea. In high summer the 'rhines' or dykes are full of lovely marsh flowers, as are the grazing meadows where the big heavy cattle move like slow barges amidst golden seas of buttercups.

I find Sedgemoor strangely mysterious and attractive and have long promised myself a solitary holiday there one day with binoculars and fishing rod. Those 'rhines' hold fish of monstrous size, great bronze carp, bream, and roach of noble girth. I do not know why I always feel that Sedgemoor is a haunted land. I never feel that about the fens of Cambridgeshire and Lincolnshire.

In the fens of the east country there are no great houses, no noble parklands, no sense of rich repose. What houses there are,

are mean and box-like, there are few fine churches, and all seem to date no earlier than Victorian times. Perhaps it is the sense I get that in the fens money is the only thing that matters. Yet the fenland people are sturdy and self reliant and the old-time wildfowlers and eel catchers rare characters, though few remain today.

And why is it that in the fens you get such noble skyscapes? Great cloud galleons drift before the winds and sunsets, which can rival those of the Highlands of Scotland. It has, I believe, something to do with the sea breezes passing over the warmer lands; I have noticed the same thing about Suffolk and the Constable country.

Coming across Suffolk the other day I realized I was in the haunts of the crossbill. Those miles and miles of Scotch firs, whole dark ranks of them along the headlands; no wonder the crossbill delights in that country. I missed my way going to Norfolk, taking a wrong turning in the fussy little town of Mildenhall, and went forty miles out of my way wandering about in the dark fastness of Thetford Forest, surely the largest forest in Britain, ranking second to Keilder.

I never realized its great size before and noticed some wonderful picnic places made by the Forestry Commission, who like the public to enjoy the beauty of their woodlands. A doctor friend who is keen on the rifle was once assailed by horrible leeches when stalking in Thetford Forest. In spring you can still hear the magical call of stone curlews about those lonely breck-lands but only in the twilight; the sound is one of the wildest and most beautiful of all bird calls.

A Rural Web

The tall dead stalks of the wild hemlock were outlined against the western sky, etched in the finest detail, and as I sat there waiting for the duck to flight I saw an amusing thing which no doubt not many would have noticed (though I say it myself), and that was that nearly every fan-like weed head was tenanted by a spider. Each had slung its web from one thin stalk to the other directly opposite, a distance I suppose of some five inches, and each spider sat motionless, exactly in the middle of the upper thread. Now I soon realised there was a purpose in this.

Being in the centre it could fasten on any incautious fly or midge which chanced to get caught in its net. They were like those fishermen on the Solway who stand for hours waiting to feel a tremor on their 'haff' nets, and, indeed these spiders were fishermen too, and with a fisherman's patience. Occasionally one would have a bite and there was a mad scramble to its prey. But only very few were lucky, even though it was a humid evening. I noticed that each spider sat in the middle of the 'top line' of the net.

It was my first night down on the riverside. My good friend Bob had given me a ring and asked me to have a flight, together with Fred Johnson, who I do believe has the gift of night sight. He can see the mallard when it is practically dark. Many a time I have been beside him, both of us staring up into the gloom, and have heard his whispered 'there goes one' and have seen nothing; only a brief 'whi! whi!' of wings told me one was past and gone.

Here I was, back in my favourite spot by the 'staunch' (as they call the river backwaters in this part of the world) sitting by the same old tree stump with the palisade of willows and tall dead weeds in front of me, with my old Polar by my side.

I could not help reflecting how right it was that each year at about this time in late autumn, that particular spot finds me there, as faithful as the green sandpiper come briefly to its chosen pool when the season comes round once again. There was no wind at all that everting, and there was no cloud. I had walked up the staunch with cautious tread in the hope of some mallard being there but the water and reeds were hidden in a vicious barrier of nettles as high as my shoulder and I could see nothing. There were no low quackings and splashings which usually betray some customers, and I had returned to my seat to watch the patient spiders.

Then at last I saw the first duck, a great band of them coming straight for me but far out of shot. They passed directly over my head in a great whispering bow and were gone. I heard no shot from Fred far up the staunch at his favourite bush, and no shot from Bob who was somewhere between us.

The stars began to prick through; it was becoming difficult to see my fellow hunters the spiders. Then silently, without quack or wing whistle, two mallard came by from left to right, the duck leading. I missed her clean, but my second shot hit the drake fair and square. He tucked in his head and fell like a rock. I heard him hit the nettle jungle on the far bank opposite, a horrible place for a retrieve for the dog has to leap from my bank into the river, swim across and scramble up the steep bank opposite where the nettles grow like a barbed wire banner.

I sent Polar, who plunged in, and I could hear him puffing, blowing and sloshing about, but I could not get him to face the stinging nettles on the far bank. After a lot of effort he came back, rolling in pain from the nettle stings on his muzzle, pushing himself along in the grass this way and that.

There was a last hope, Bob and his good retriever, who was farther along the staunch. Alas! his old Betsy, who has retrieved me many a duck from this very place, has now become too old and deaf, and he has another bitch, which, though good indeed, has not the courage and persistence of old Betsy. However, Bob appeared out of the dusk and volunteered to get her over, which he did, after a tremendous lot of urging and throwing of sticks. She spent some time in the water, then at last climbed the bank among the nettles. Then all fell silent. There was no sound of her in the water nor among the weeds; she had gone over the top of the bank on to the dark field opposite.

We waited for some time. At last she came back, but alas! without my drake. We realized that the night was to be a blank, for neither Bob nor Fred had had a fair chance. I went next morning and had another search but the cover was too thick. The drake may have fallen on top of the huge beds of bull rushes which choke the stream, great beds of them lying horizontally.

The loss of a single bird under these conditions where, unlike a flight pond one has several good chances at flight, is always doubly annoying and I left, feeling as though a five-pound brown trout had gone off with my cast. To bag a couple of duck on these outings is reckoned a triumph, for they are all truly wild birds, none of your half-tame reared mallard. So it was back to the Land-Rover and the bumpy ride up the narrow lane, with rabbits bobbing about in the headlights and a startled bird blinded by the glare dodging about in front of the bonnet.

As for that fat toad I brought back from Norfolk and which I saw crawl away under the dying ferns, I hope I may see or hear him again for I have an affection for toads, who are far more intelligent than many people think and are always ready to make friends if you can offer a fat worm now and then by way of introducing yourself.

Referring once more to spiders, I am one of those people who have an unreasoning distaste for them and cannot pick one up. If, as often happens, one falls into the bath, I have to enlist my daughter's help to come and pick it out. There are also, in my old house, spiders which seem as big as tarantulas, enormous creatures with a two-inch leg span which move with tremendous speed across the carpet and which I swear could give you a nasty bite; indeed there is a species of hunting spider which lives mostly in gardens which bit the thumb of a cleric of my acquaintance and sent him to hospital. Can you wonder I view these creatures with distaste?

Yet those little patient fishermen, waiting on their webs by the dusky river, filled me with admiration, and I felt quite a fellow feeling for them. Which reminds me, that many years ago my wife purchased a bunch of bananas and in the centre she discovered a mother spider with a mighty brood of youngsters which she defended with upraised legs and champing jaws. It was a nasty looking furry creature of vivid hue and had evidently had a long sea voyage from some far distant clime, but was prepared to defend her offspring to the death.

Wren Song

All last spring and summer I listened in vain for that resounding jubilant song of the wren, a song which is out of all proportion to the diminutive vocalist. Every year they used to have a nest somewhere in my garden, usually in the close-hugging dark foliage of an Irish Yew.

This departure of one of my favourite guests filled me with sorrow. And then, a week ago, as I lay in bed at seven a.m., summoning enough courage to get up, I had a pleasant surprise. I had my bedroom window just open, the curtains were drawn back and I was watching the last surviving leaf of my Virginia creeper wagging on the pane. Suddenly, into the bedroom popped a jenny wren. It perched on the sill and gave the inside of the window the once over, for spiders are the mainstay of the wren's diet at the beginning of winter.

What a joy it was to see again that cheeky little stub tail, cheeky as that of a working terrier. It did not tarry long and the next moment it flew out again.

That little bird had probably come from far away, maybe from some southern county where the hard weather of last winter was not so fierce as in the Midlands and the north.

As wrens band together in winter in their favourite roost (purely for the sake of warmth, for at other times they are not gregarious), the coming winter may be a crucial time for these gallant little birds. It is truly a case of the more the merrier with our common wrens if they are not to perish from hypothermia. For some reason the more diminutive goldcrest does not seem to suffer so much as the brown wren; maybe because it is a hunter of the great coniferous woodlands and perhaps fares better. Little is known of the roosting habits of the goldcrest or firecrest.

At the beginning of this month I paid a visit to a very beautiful private lake in the Midlands and spent an enjoyable afternoon watching a great concourse of wildfowl. Mallard and golden eye were disporting in the shallows, tufters bobbed about like black and white corks and fleets of Canadas swam and grazed, making noises like stones rattled in tin cans.

But what I enjoyed watching most through my powerful Ziess glasses was a band of some thirty greylags, some truly wild birds, which were sitting at ease on a bank some hundred yards distant from me. The late autumn sun shone warm upon them, as it did on the golden and red chestnuts on the far side of the lake.

Many of my old friends sat with in-tucked orange bills, their eyes closed, showing the pale membrane. These looked blissfully contented in the warm sun, laziness and happiness personified. Others stood with upraised heads, their keen brown eyes ever alert for anything suspicious, a wariness born of thousands of years of persecution. Some yawned, others fanned their broad wings over outstretched paddles, some preened, but most slept.

Occasionally a greylag would call from the lake, then every head would be raised, listening. One or two old birds, having slept, got up and rolled forward with a nautical gait common to all the 'paddled' duck and goose tribe, the body swaying from side to side. This rolling gait gives the goose great dignity, majesty even.

I sometimes wonder when I am looking at wild geese like this how I can ever bring myself to shoot one. Nor would I under those conditions. It is a different matter when they are flighting at dawn, coming in from the sand bars. They are ready for me, I am ready for them. I wondered where some of those geese had been bred, It seemed to me unlikely they were Icelandic or Spitzbergen birds. It is far more probable that they had been bred in the Norfolk marshes or maybe the outer Isles of northern Scotland. Some I know breed around the lake itself but each year they are joined by truly wild birds, just as they are in the Severn Wildfowl Trust.

That afternoon was one of those rare days we get just at

the onset of winter when, for a time at least, the tide seems to recede. It was warm enough for me to discard my coat. I leant my elbows on the wall where ivy grew, and upon the late flowers many wasps and bees were busy, as well as hover flies and bluebottles, all feasting on the last of the summer wine.

The gold and saffron colours in the trees on the far shore seemed almost out of place on that warm and tranquil after-noon, for even the grass was not yet winter-bitten and dead. Where the geese rested it was green as summer. Occasionally one of them would lazily pluck at it with its heavy orange bill. No other of our British geese has the thick furrowed neck and heavy build of the greylag. There is little to distinguish them from farmyard geese save for their alert and stately carriage.

They kept apart from the larger Canadas. The latter are perhaps the most handsome of all the British geese, yet they do not excite me any more than the French partridge compared to our brown partridge. Incidentally, the latter really seems to be making something of a comeback in the Midlands, but I doubt whether they will ever become as common as once they were. I have yet to see a really large covey. The sprays that kill all those little minty weeds they delighted in have seen to that.

One goose among the company of greylags puzzled me, for it had the build of a greylag but had a plain drab-grey body and its head and neck were pure white. I contacted the owner of the lake and he told me that it was believed to be a cross between a snow goose and a greylag, for several greylags had been seen 'attending' a snow goose earlier in the season. Like so many hybrids it was not nearly so attractive as the genuine article.

The same applies to other hybrids. Bird fanciers, especially those interested in the finch tribe, strive to cross bullfinches with canaries, and goldfinches with bramblings, and are up to all sorts of tricks. Yet the result is never so attractive as the original colour pattern and the goldfinch-canary hybrid is a thing of naught. We can juggle Nature's colours and patterns about like meddlesome monkeys, but the results are never satisfactory except perhaps in the case of horses and dogs, and even there we breed some dog monstrosities with noses so 'squashed in' the poor animals can hardly breathe.

One of the most delicate and charming of all our wild geese is the lesser whitefront which was, some fifty years ago, considered a great rarity. Now most wildfowl collections can boast having a pair or so, and one I am thinking of in Bedfordshire has a large gaggle of lessers. The strangest of all the wild geese in this country is the brent goose which is tubby, small, and has an almost reptilian head.

I read in my paper that farmers on the east coast, driven desperate by the attentions of the brents on their winter wheat, are providing mown grassland between the coast and their crops. But knowing wild geese as I do, the brent will welcome this with cackles of glee, for a wild goose likes nothing more than a change of diet. It will be able to have a belly full of sweet grass and then go over on to the winter wheat for 'afters'. The only remedy is the gun or netting. There is no reason now why some shooting of brents should not be allowed. Like the barnacle they benefited enormously by protection, though on the table I doubt whether they can match the greylag.

Owls and Others

The small boy in my village who is a keen bird watcher has not seen any more of his kestrel which escaped the other day, soon after he brought it for all to see. This is a terrible blow to him. It was one of his prize possessions. Apparently it had been scared by some children who rattled its flight cage and the door, being insecurely shut, sprang open and the bird escaped.

These delightful members of the hawk tribe seemed to be unaffected by the poisonous sprays which killed the sparrow-hawk and peregrine. And as is well known, the construction of the big motorways have helped, for pedestrians are absent and so are the farmers' sprays. The wide margins and embankments teem with mice and voles, and often there are vantage points, fence posts and trees, where they can rest and watch, for the kestrel does not always rely on hovering. It will spend hours on a rock waiting for mice to move below.

Now that the mating season of the forest owls is upon us, amusing things are happening o'nights around the boy's aviary where he has a pair of tawny owls (rescued originally from a hollow tree when the mother was found dead, probably shot by some lout with a gun). One night, the boy tells me, nine owls were gathered on the neighbouring roof tops and chimneys, hooting away in a regular owls' choir. A lady in the village told me she liked to hear them when they chose her roof ridge, and she hooted back at them up the chimney. When she did this there was an uncanny pause, no answering hoot, but astonished silence. One can imagine the owl peering down the dark hole of the chimney wondering how on earth one of his brethren had got down there.

Walking in the forest the other day the boy told me he heard a party of jays setting up a terrific racket. He stole close along the path and saw two magnificent long-eared owls sitting side by side in a fir tree. The jays were mobbing them. What maddens me is that so far I have yet to see a long-eared owl in our forest, yet I know these noble birds are about because other keen students of birds beside the boy have seen them. It is our only version of the noble eagle owl of the Canadian woods; its long ears give it a most fierce and dignified appearance, and it's a big owl too.

I suppose that the snowy owl is the most handsome of the owl family, though they have not the large luminous eyes of the eagle owl or tawny. I was looking at a pair in Lilford Park recently, most dignified birds.

I always think the owl family is quite unbirdlike with its eyes to the front and with its goblin face. They move, also, in a strange unbirdlike manner, bobbing and turning, their heads revolving. Their wonderful harmonious plumage matches the tough wood in the decaying oaks; there are streaks of lichen- grey and all shades of umber, sienna, and deep Vandyck brown.

If we had to think up a suitable cry for this night-loving fowl, we could not better the resonant hollow hooting which is somehow exactly right. The thin prolonged screech of the white owl hardly matches it. We rarely see the short-eared owl here, but round the rough grass margins of the inland reservoirs in Northamptonshire I have seen them hunting, for it is a daylight hunter.

Up to a few years ago the greater spotted woodpecker was a daily visitor to my bird table in winter but I have not seen one now for some years. It was a common bird in the Midland oak woods and is still there, for I heard one last spring when I was waiting for pigeon to come to roost.

My moorhen family are settling down on my Big Pond. I like to hear them say 'goodnight' to me when I put on my bedroom light', it is a cheerful friendly 'cruick' uttered once or twice.

In the early mornings when it is getting light I hear scuffles on the pond, loud splashes and a rare old commotion. This is usually triggered off by one of the former brood attempting to revisit its birthplace. The old birds will have none of it, and terrific chases occur all over the garden. With lowered bills held rigid like rapiers and with their black feathers fluffed out, they charge the trespasser who eventually takes wing.

One strange thing I have noticed is that they do not roost on the pond as formerly but up in a birch tree close by. It may be there has been a fox about for lately I have heard one barking on the forest edge just as dusk began to cloak the fields.

Foxes are common in the forest, and though the Woodland Pytchley gives them a run for their money, master Charles James usually leads them a fine old dance in around the woods and rarely goes away. The bark of a dog fox is a strange, rather eerie sound, a sort of wheezy cough which carries a long distance over the dimming fields. Different indeed to the terrible agonizing cry of a vixen or a badger, which will guarantee to stand your hair on end if heard in the silence of night. I often think that foxes bay the moon like dogs and wolves. I had a black retriever once who always bayed the moon when it was at the full, and it was a habit I never broke him of. It is akin to the chiming of hounds in kennel.

Speaking of foxhounds reminds me of the old story of the hunt servant being eaten up by them when he went into the kennels one night (all that remained of him, so the story goes, were his boots). This has never been substantiated. I remember Major Paget, who knew more about the history of hounds and hunting than most men, telling me that it was a complete fable, and he should know.

Incidentally I had dinner with him only a week or so before he was himself killed out hunting. Strangely enough, that night we were talking about foxes and hunting and somehow the conversation turned to more serious things. 'There is only one way I wish to die', he said, 'and that is in the hunting field'. A day or so later he broke his neck jumping a hedge into a road. It is a wonder more people are not killed hunting.

I had a farmer friend who was a keen follower of the Pytchley and who was an excellent judge of a horse, and of a hound (and a man also, for he had a fine war record). One winter day I was motoring along a country road near his farm and I saw, far away across several fields a galloping horse dragging something behind it on the ground. I saw, too, a man running and on the wind came terrible cries. It was my farmer friend who had been dragged. His foot had caught in the stirrup and he was ripped to ribbons and died that night.

I have been dragged myself when I was a boy, my foot having been caught in the stirrup, and though my ordeal lasted only a matter of minutes before my foot came free, I shall never forget that awful feeling of helplessness and the terrible jarring and banging as I was dragged along. Luckily my foot came out of the stirrup; never again did I ride with my feet right home.

November Days

It is a sad moment for me when I reach up to the garage shelf and take down the glass pane which fits the door. It is through this small opening that my beloved swallows fly in and out during the summer days, the same father swallow which sits outside my window in May and sings his praises to the dawn. I wonder where he is now, and pray that he has made a safe passage of the Alps and not finished up in some greasy foreign belly. This afternoon I put the pane back in place and fastened it securely.

It was last April that I welcomed my swallows home and straightaway took out the pane. They prefer a small aperture through which to fly to their nests. I tried one year leaving the doors wide open in the daytime but the sparrows went in. They do not like venturing into a darkened garage, they know they cannot make a quick getaway, and if I catch them in there I shoot them. They know this. The common house sparrow is an intelligent bird; it has found the best way to survive in all parts of the world. It is tough and will eat almost anything.

Well, it is a long haul to the time of the swallow, to those quiet evenings when I watch the sky and mistake every distant starling for a swallow, for their flight is very similar. In actual fact, the late summer was a good one in our part of the world for them; my friend Bob Gent had a full quota in his barns. This is strange, as we had such a dreary time with grey skies and storms of wind and rain, winds so strong that they blew over my larvae cage and damaged one of the growing sallows therein. I shall not be taken unawares again. I have stayed the cage from each four corners with stout nylon cord fastened to tent pegs.

I am hampered when I want to paint, for I need the daylight. At times I am seized with great ideas for pictures, smooth mudbanks of Solwayside with all their delicate sheeny tints of blue and grey and violet, with the bright creeks winding, and wildfowl on the wing. Often I turn again and again to another favourite subject of mine, a bullfinch pair in a winter hedge with dew drops on the purple thorns, and maybe two or three pinkish hips matching the breast of the cock bird.

I know that gardeners loathe the bullfinch for the mischief they do in the spring, when they visit the blossoming apples and cherries for the half-open buds. These make a delicious change for them after the dreary days of winter when the only berries they can find are those of the honeysuckle. Those newly opened apple-blossom buds must be to them like the first fresh lettuce is to us.

My little hen bullfinch, rescued survivor from a drowned-out nestful some years ago, regards me as her mate. She sings to me to attract attention for, like all females, she will not tolerate neglect. She looks into my eye with her little brown one, with the lid just closed a little, which is a sign of trust and content-ment in a bird. The eye is truly the window of the inner life spirit and I wonder what she sees? Is it some vast cock bullfinch, hardly! She sees someone who has known her since her eyes first opened, the bringer of food, but I see there something more. She and I, both alive, and linked in spirit. Some who read these lines will snort and sneer. Let them, I write what I feel about nature.

The song thrushes suffer the most in bitter weather for they will not eat bread like the blackbird, but they will eat apples, and I am delighted to inform all bird lovers that song thrushes will eat chick crumbs. These can be bought at any pet shop and they seem to suit them well. I have always found it a problem with all the thrush family, redwings and fieldfares included, for the latter suffer dreadfully in hard frost and many die.

The other night the phone rang and a friend asked me to shoot a mallard down by the river. It wasn't a good evening for duck, no wind at all and the day had been mild. Also this 'back end' has been bad for duck in my part of the Midlands and the wigeon have not yet come in. Up this particular river valley with which readers must be now familiar, where the mists crawl at evening and the peewits wail in the dusk, the wigeon companies feed on the water-meadows. Like wild geese they have their favourite pastures year after year where perhaps there is a certain flavour of spray-free mints, those tiny plants like clover and others which love the damp terrain.

I got behind my favourite willow stump, which I have mentioned before. The tree has been dead these many years, indeed I do not remember it standing. In front is the 'staunch', the backwater which takes off some of the violent floods, and on the opposite side that horrible sheer bank thick with those very tall vicious nettles whose smarting sting will last a week. The dogs hate to get a bird from that side and where possible we take the duck as they cross the staunch, no easy matter.

I did not think I should get a shot. There were the usual dancing gnats which showed how mild it was, the occasional 'cruik' of a moorhen in the reeds, the splash of a fish. I looked for the bat which usually flitters round at this quiet hour, but all I saw was a cock reed-bunting which came and perched on a dead rod of willow herb and peered at me, wondering what on earth I was. Its inquisitive little face made me smile. It leant forward on the weed and peered and peered, and then flew off.

The sun was well down before I saw the first mallard. They were as small as starlings in a compact bunch, heading away on a definite line, some barley stubble perhaps not yet under the plough. I watched them dwindle into the sunset. Polar, my lab, gave a muffled squeak. I looked round. He was half raising himself on his back legs like a hare and was staring across the misty field behind us. There was an old cock pheasant 'walking in'. Further up the staunch are some big old leaning willows and some thorn bushes. That was to be its dormitory for the night.

The light was going so fast now I could barely make out the far dim shape, and soon the shadows swallowed it up. Then, some five minutes later, I heard it crow *cock! cock! cock!* Listening carefully I heard a reply from far down the river. It was now almost dark, and soon I should see the lights of Bob's Land-Rover come jolting down the rutty field track to pick me up.

I was just about to gather Polar and unload my gun when I saw a dim speeding blur on my right. I had number seven in my gun, really too small a shot for duck, which are fairly tough birds. The gun swung up, there was a brief stab of flame, followed by a bump out in the field. I unleashed the hound and he was off into the dark to come back puffing and huffing with a fine mallard drake in his mouth. I saw the white wing bar and thought at first it was a duck but when I looked close I saw the dark madder breast, almost black in the bad light, and the dark neck and head of a drake.

We went back up the track and saw the rabbits hopping in the headlights and a trundling hedgehog crossed in front of us and vanished in the hedge. The mild weather had brought him out, but he was in peril, for numberless hedgehogs are caught out in late autumn when frost follows a mild spell. And as we journeyed homewards towards a cosy farmhouse tea which Bob's pretty wife and daughters had prepared for us, I wondered where I should be in a few days' time on my trail of the grey geese.

At Autumn's End

All the signs that winter is about my igloo are patently obvious. At an unearthly hour the other day the sweep arrived, summoned by my daughter (what male ever thinks of sweeps?), and mysterious rumblings sounded from the belly of my chimney, for who, with any sense of the comforts of this life, can do without an open fire? Town-dwellers are, I understand, not allowed coal or wood fires, so they would not miss them. But, for me, an open flame is a bit of outdoor wildness right there in the hearth, the glowing apple log, the fragrant smoke, the golden fiery caverns burning there in the old dog grate under the wide chimney piece which has the date of my house carved upon it (1660). Charles the Second was about then if I remember aright, Pepys was writing his diary, and the fire of London and the plague were all about that time.

Sweeps are a vanishing race even in the country. I remember the sweep at my old home. He came at six, and the servants were ready for him, the carpets covered in dust sheets. He came with a small grubby dog in a basket and it took him an hour or more to sweep the many chimneys. He was so old he remembered the time when boys were sent up to climb the chimneys to dislodge the soot. Across the road at the Hall there was a brass plate let into the chimney piece which warned against any boy being sent up, as one got stuck and, I believe, perished. After doing the chimneys our sweep was given breakfast by the staff and I well remember being frightened at the sight of the coal-black little man, the whites of his eyes making him appear like a startled negro.

That time after a day's shoot, with my dog lying before the fire weary with his day in the open air, and with a good meal disposed of (for both of us) and perhaps a glass of the hard stuff beside me and a pipe drawing well, these are true countryman's pleasures.

Other signs are everywhere manifest of the passing year. Only a single green apple remains at the top of my old tree on the lawn; a few late fallings provide daily provender for hunting blackbirds. Big Pond is roofed with rafts of fallen leaves, birch and willow, balsam poplar and hawthorn. A fragrant blue whisp drifts over my bonfire of summer rubbish, the old michaelmas daisy rods, potato haulms, and dead leaves.

My garden robin pipes his *triste* song of the Fall, though not I fancy with his old vigour. All the stubbles have gone under and the big fields by the forest have been sown long since.

They look as tidy as a well-kept garden, for the man who farms them is an expert. He has drained the low-lying fields by the brook and his crops delight the eye of every good husbandman; even I, who dislike too tidy a landscape, can appreciate them. The trees have unloaded their last leaves with the recent frosts, one day the ashes were full and next day the dead leaves lay thickly on lane and field, felled in a single night. Only the oaks retain their foliage, and my beech hedge.

A kind reader of my recent memoirs *A Child Alone*, having read about the old timbered Hall in Shropshire where generations ago my family lived, sent me three little oak saplings from the park. One I have trained into a Bonzai, or rather I hope to make a Bonzai of it. I look at it with sad jealousy, for if it is correctly tended it will be alive long after I have departed from the scene. Do not think I am getting morbid, but I look with secret envy on the oaks. Would I could have their span of life in a world which, despite the efforts of man to wreck it, yet retains for me unimaginable loveliness.

There is that softness and gentleness about the distant fields and forest now that summer has gone and autumn nearly so, a faint mist which gathers at evening and is loth to depart at midday. And when the nights are still I like to hear the grunts of the fallow bucks pursuing their bashful does along the forest rides. For I live in a part of the Midlands where great ancient woods are all about me, many of them of oak but, alas, too many now of fir. Coming over the high ground above the hamlet you can see the forest stretching out all along the horizon, home of fallow deer and the little muntjac.

On silent nights, when the wind has gone and the moon rises over the dark trees, huge and rose-red in the early mists, I can hear the clarion crowings of the cock pheasants, one answering the other, and often too the asthmatic cough of a dog fox, who like the fallow bucks feels the urge for feminine company. High up among the stars, the sorrowful single pipe of travelling golden plover is often heard, and the wild call of curlew heading for the Wash or Severnside. Rarely, alas, do I hear that most thrilling sound of all, the clamour of wild geese, for they seldom come this way now, though less than forty years ago the whitefronts came regularly to the river valley over the hill.

Their favourite haunt, to which they came year after year, is now one shining expanse of water, for under the sweet grass (which no doubt contained some special flavour which appealed to goosey palates) there is a gravel stratum. In time all this valley will no doubt be water. Unfortunately gravel pits are usually too deep for wildfowl, which must have shallows and plenty of reeds. But they form good harbours for coarse fish. Every weekend there are lines of cars belonging to workers from all over the industrial Midlands. And what a blessing this is for them, to be away from the turmoil of the factory bench to the peace of the waterside!

It is places like this which will be supremely important in the years to come, when everyone will have more leisure time. The coming of the silicon chip will mean a fuller life for many, and though there is much truth in Joe Gormley's statement that man was not born to spend all his days in factory or office, some work is necessary for a happy life, even if it is for three days a week. I can see the time coming when sensible people who, having learnt to use their leisure time correctly, mostly I hope in the open air, can lead much more enjoyable and healthy lives. The sooner that time comes the better. I have no use for anyone who does not work (when work is available) and despise those who spend their whole lives in pursuit of pleasure. There are drones in society at both ends of the social scale.

On the fifth of October I paid a last visit to Rutland Water, this time without a fishing rod. This man-made inland sea has been landscaped as beautifully as any by that great master of landscape design in the eighteenth century, Capability Brown.

On that golden autumn afternoon, the great sweep of glittering water, with its two great arms, one to the south and one to the north, lay riffling under a gentle westerly wind. Among the hanging woods some trees were showing golden flames. Mercifully, most of the trees are oaks and ash; a few dead stricken elms marred the scene, those dreadful diseased skeletons which make some parts of the Midlands as gaunt and bare as in midwinter. In the shallows, mallard and coots were disporting and throwing the water about in silver drops. Fishermen's craft seen far out looked like those paper boats made by children; some were on the move, leaving a bright spear of light in their wake.

There are four main picnic places laid out around the reservoir. The most beautiful of all is at Barnsdale on the north bank. Here the entrance road dives down through hanging woods of oak which, in spring, are floored with sheets of bluebell and fern.

If ever there was a pleasure park more suited to that era which is coming, when people will have more leisure time, then Rutland Water must surely take pride of place. I am sure Keilder Forest will never equal it even when the great reservoir is completed, which will be slightly larger than Rutland Water. The undulating hills and valleys which descend fold on fold to the water's edge are of great beauty, and where trees were absent others have been planted in groves and ribbons near the winding shores. Even the public lavatories are of splendid design and do not disfigure the landscape. On the southern shore stand the remains of the eighteenth-century church, nothing to boast about before the water came, but which now stands like a light-house with its chancel floor filled up with concrete, so that it is above the level of the water.

Great waves can arise on this inland sea. Not long since, I went there on a day of great winds which were more than gale force. The white rollers were breaking over the wails of the church and charging at the shore, a wind so powerful it was almost impossible to stand against it. Even in a moderate wind it can be like voyaging on the open sea, as I found when fishing there around midsummer. But the fishing boats are sturdy and diesel-driven and very seaworthy, though on that day of gales all were safely tied by their noses to the fishing pier.

Wintersweet

I write this on a day of unseasonable calm. No wind stirs the surface of Big Pond, sending those exquisite intermittent ripples across the pale expanse over which a mist lies like a veil. The hollows in the fields are misty too, and Far Forest barely visible. Only a few days remain to Christmas. In the village stores cotton-wool blobs of snow suspended on strings try to convey the atmosphere of Yuletide, but snow seems far away.

High on a topmost twig of the apple tree at the top of the garden a song thrush was fluting, trying out a few tentative staves. He sang in a half-hearted manner, I thought, with none of the vigour of spring. Perhaps he felt, as I did, something of the soothing quiet of this late December afternoon, but his vocal efforts gave no hint of spring to my mind. Only the early black-bird's warble can do that, and they will not be singing until February.

To the west and low down there is a luminous light where the sun was, but I have seen no sunlight today, only this soft mist which adds such mystery to field and wood. By my back door a wintersweet is in full bloom, its bright yellow stars, bursting magically from the shiny green stems, seem to light the gloomy day. When I first came to my present house I foolishly planted a clematis which soon ran riot all over the bittersweet and complete hid it. Though the pale pink flowers were pretty enough in summer, I came to miss those yellow stars of the evergreen. So I rooted the clematis out in the autumn and now I am rewarded by this yellow flaming bush. How strange that it should flower at this dead time of the year!

Across the misty ploughland opposite, a sly pheasant crept across, making for the forest, pecking as he went, pausing here and there to sample something, and a band of green plover manoeuvred about like guardsmen, their rounded wings beating in unison. There is beauty in winter as there is at all seasons of the year and these soft mild days have great charm.

Removing the front of my purple emperor cage to check on my sleeping babies I found to my dismay that two had somehow left the sallow tree on which they are hibernating and had chosen the damp and grubby muslin for their winter rest. How they got there I could not think, as the tree is banded with grease and cotton wool. I can only think they must have been on the leaves and had fallen off clear of the grease band. To leave them there would be to court disaster so I set about the infinitely delicate job of restoring them to the tree. Their companions, some dozen or more, have been good larvae and chosen the usual hibernating sites, either close to a sallow bud or in the crutch of the tree where a branch protrudes. How to do it, that was the problem!

Both larvae appeared to be in their winter coma and the utmost care would have to be taken so as not to damage their frail bodies in any way. I got a leaf and very gently pushed it under the head of each baby. They immediately began to wave their horns about, which was a good sign. If the weather had been frosty they would not have moved. With the utmost care and patience I coaxed them on to the leaf. The hardest part came when I reached the tail, for the larva attaches itself to its choice seat by a silken pad.

By degrees I got them on the leaf and then transferred that to the main stem of the sallow, attaching the leaf by a binding wire. After about half an hour I was delighted to see one of them crawl on to the dark stem of the sallow and join six others who were all side by side in a lower crutch like boys in a dormitory. I have noticed that these infant larvae like the company of their fellows.

Once in position they are almost impossible to see, for the colour of their diminutive bodies exactly matches the winter sallow bark. It was strange to think of the day to come, in the heat of high summer, when those insignificant little creatures would be in quite a different guise in full glory of purple scaled

wing and with all the vast rich forest at their disposal, hard even to think that that distant naked misty forest would ever shimmer in the July heat with its uncountable millions of humming flies. My little charges safely put to bed, I closed the door to the cage with great satisfaction, for the operation had been a perilously delicate one.

My song thrush was still singing high on his perch, outlined now against the fast-setting sun. The dusk came down with tropical suddenness. Soon Far Forest was swallowed in mist and I distinctly heard the coughing bark of a fox somewhere over there among the dark firs and naked oaks. He would be setting out on his hunting no doubt. Maybe also the unusually mild weather had set alight the embers of love, though it is later on, in February and March, that foxes start running the vixens in earnest.

In a very short time now the year will be ended, a year which, for me, has been so full of delight and interest in this unbelievably beautiful world, delights which so many millions would think of no account, but which to me are the very stuff of existence. This enormous ball of the world, riding relentlessly through the immensities of space, rich beyond all imagining in natural beauty, is taking us away from the sun, yet in a week or less the sun will be returning, Christmas will be over and done, the turkey carcass will be suspended from the old apple tree for the tits and starlings, and I shall be listening for the first low warble of the cock blackbirds. The little mud cups in the upper beams of my garage will once again be tenanted by my resident swallows and the whole panorama of nature's year will begin again.